HOMELESS

HOMELESS

Rodney D Miranda

HOMELESS

iUniverse books may be ordered through booksellers or by contacting:

iUniverse
1663 Liberty Drive
Bloomington, IN 47403
www.iuniverse.com
1-800-Authors (1-800-288-4677)

ISBN: 978-1-5320-5146-3 (sc)
ISBN: 978-1-5320-5147-0 (e)

Library of Congress Control Number: 2018908921

Print information available on the last page.

iUniverse rev. date: 07/27/2018

CHAPTER 1

John was a young businessman born into wealth. His parents owned a real estate and a software company that designed software for the military. John was next in line to take over his parents' business and become one of the richest people in the United States. He had a wife, Nicole, and a young daughter, Marri. He was the happiest person in the world because he had everything a young successful man could ask for.

John did everything with his family and put nobody above them. Some people would say he was a selfish, arrogant person and only thought about himself, his family, and his father's company. His father taught John everything he knew on how to run a company and make a lot of money, but one thing he didn't have was a childhood. Growing up He never for to play or do sports, instead his father taught him business. John only had a few more years to go before his father would let him take over the multibillion-dollar organization. He believed that only hard work would get you to where you needed to be in life, and dedicated his adult life to be successful.

Over a period of tiime he become a huge public figure, he known all over the world because he designed software programs for cell phones and computers for the military. A lot of people who worked for him didnt like him as a person, but respected him because he was a very powerfully man. He would never give any back to his community or even give change to a homeless people. He would drive by people in his very expensive sports car while they would be holding up a sign saying "Anything would help" and "God bless," and he would just roll up his window or tell them to get a job and keep driving. He would never tell people "thank you" or anything to make them feel like they were doing anything right., because he didn't know any better. He didnt know what's it's like to struggle or go without a meal.

John loved his family and his business more than anything in the world. Hos wife and his daughter were the lights of his life. For a year, Nicole had been strangely sick, in and out of the hospital's but doctors hadn't been able to find the source of what was making her ill. He just did his best to be the best husband and father he could be for his wife and to comfort her through this sickness until the doctors could find out what was wrong.

A few more months went by, and he could see his wife's condition getting worse by the day. They finally found a doctor in another part of the world that thought he knew what was wrong with her. So they took some time off work to go see this physician.

When they got there, the doctor told them that he wanted to run one more last to make sure he knew what was wrong and it would take a few weeks, and they would have to stay there and wait for the results to come back. During the process of finding out, John took Nicole to explore the beautiful surroundings of another country, treating her to whatever her heart desired. John was a great husband to his wife. His life was empty without her and his daughter in his life.

Now the time had come to find out what was wrong with his wife. Doctors told them that she had a very rare type of brain cancer that only less than one hundred people in the world had, but nobody had survived it. They told her she had less than six months, if she were lucky, and then she would die. Both of them were couldn't believe what they were hearing. His wife, his best friend, and his world was going to die and he couldn't do anything to help her. The only thing he could do was to keep his wife happy until the day came that she would be gone.

When they got back to California and let their families know what was going on. John decided to take the next six months off work to keep his wife comfortable until she passed. He just wanted to keep her happy and do whatever he could for her. So they took trips to all the places she wanted to go all over the world.

For two months straight, they traveled until they got tired of it, but all she wanted to do after they saw everything was stay at home for the rest of her days and be at peace with her family. John did everything he could, but he could see that she was depressed and letting the cancer get to her. He would get up every morning, make her breakfast in bed, and help her take a shower to get her day going. He'd try to take her out to get some fresh air, but sometimes she couldn't even get out of bed. It hurt him to see his wife go through this, he never prayed to God and never believed in him before this, but he didn't know what else to do at this point, so he prayed and prayed that she would get better.

A few more months went by, and Nicole had gotten even worse. Now she needed two people to get her out of bed, and she stopped eating. So the doctors put a feeding tube in her so she could eat. John became a very angry man, blaming everybody, even God, for what was happening to his wife. He knew that her last days were coming soon and all he could is watch her suffer and go throw the pain.

One morning, she woke him up and asked him to get her some water because she was very thirsty. He got up and went in the kitchen got a big glass of water. When he got back into the room, he put the glass of water on the side table by her bed.

He asked her, "Do you need help sitting up to drink?"

She didn't answer him, so he got closer and saw that her eyes were closed. He thought she must have gone back to sleep. He decided to call her name and wake her up so she could get some water, but she still didn't say anything.

Now he was concerned about her, so he shook her gently, saying, "Babe, I got your water you asked for."

Still there was nothing. He finally decided to check for a pulse, and he couldn't find one. The time came that he was hoping wouldn't. She was gone, and he was heart broken. He yelled for her to come back and not to give up, but it was too late. She knew that she was going to die so she sent him to get his some water so he wouldn't see her die.

An hour went by of him crying and screaming for his wife. All he could do was just lay in the bed and hold her body until the ambulance got there to take her away from him.

CHAPTER 2

The pain that he was feeling was to much for him to bare. He had lost his best friend, his wife, and his light, and nobody but his daughter could help the pain go away, and even that was just enough to get by the rest of the day.

Days went by, and John didn't have the strength to get out of bed, he didn't know what to do with himself. He would sleep with pictures of his wife and cry himself to sleep. His coworkers from work started coming around, trying to help him get up and at least move around, but John just wasn't feeling like living any more. He just layed in bed not wanted to do anything at all.

One day, his daughter came in the room with some orange juice. "Dad, it's nice outside. Do you think you could push me on the swing?"

He looked her in her eyes, and all he could think was how much of her mom she had in her. "Yes, baby, I will get up and be the best father to you as I can be."

As he was swinging her on the swing, he was telling her, "I'm sorry for not being there for you in the past few days. I just really miss your mother. He also told her, no matter what happens, I will never leave you.

John told his father he wanted to take a few weeks off work so he could plan for the funeral and just try to get back at enjoying life like he once used to. So a few more days went by, and it was time for him to get everything ready for the funeral. He had to go see his wife before they buried her. He got in the room where she was at and just broke down. He saw Nicole laying on a table all dressed up in a beautiful dress and make up done. She looked like she was just sleeping.

He still couldn't believe that she wasn't alive and just wished she would come back to him and Marri. He held her hand, crying his eyes out and telling her, "I will do everything I can to take care of our daughter. I will not let anything or anyone harm her."

The next day, he had the funeral. Over two hundred people from both sides of the family showed up to show their love and support to John and Marri. He couldn't even recognize most of them because they mostly all knew his dad and worked or did business with him. He felt so alone because he realized that he really had no friends or anybody to talk to besides his daughter.

Another week went by, and it was time for John to go back to work and focus on taking over his father's business and building a stronger relationship with his clients to gain their trust when it came time to take over. He decided it was time to start making new friends at work and hang out with people he wouldn't normally go out with.

One day, he was talking to a guy named Frank, who was about the same age as he was.

He asked frank, would you like to go to the bar to talk about business and your future in the company?"

Frank said, "Sure, but can my friend, Derek, come? He's a lawyer."

John said, "Sure. The more, the better."

So after a long day's work at the office, Frank recommended they go to a local bar that he went to a few times a week. Once they got there, Derek was already waiting and had a few drinks lined up too. They had a great night just talking about business, sports, kids, life, and a bunch of other things.

John started to feel better about everything, and he was actually having a good time. He took a cab home because he had a few drinks in him, and when he got home, he saw Marri was still up, waiting for him.

He told her, "I made a few friends at work and had a great time."

She could see that her dad was smiling, something she hadn't seen in a while. So she was happy too.

The next day at work, Frank came up to him. "Did you have a good time out?"

John said, "Yes, it was an awesome night. I needed that. Would you and Derek want to go to a basketball game with me on an upcoming Friday night?"

Frank said, "I'd love to go. I'll have to ask Derek if he would like to go."

Later that day, Derek told Frank that he would love to go. After frank told john that they were in, he made a phone call to get floor seats for the Friday's game. This time, John chose not to drink so he could drive to the game. He showed up in one of his super nice luxury cars to pick up the guys for the game, he also got VIP passes to go in the locker room to meet the players before the game.

Frank and Derek were so surprised that John was doing this for them.

Frank told him, "Everyone at work doesn't think too highly of you. They all think you're all about yourself and money

John said, "I really never had any friends growing up because my father wanted me to follow in his footsteps. When I asked to play outside or go places, my dad would tell me no and say I needed to start worrying about running a business than running around and playing." He told them that he never had any friends growing up. When I wanted to go play basketball or just go outside my father wouldn't allow me to go out and do anything.

Frank felt sorry that John never really had a childhood friend or was able to do things as young kid, So he told John, "From here on out, I will be your friend."

For the first time in his life, John felt excited to have a friend he could talk to and count on. John knew that Frank already had a friend, Derek and didn't want to come between them.

He didn't want to split them up, so he told Frank, "Whenever we go out to do things, Derek should come too."

John has a strange feeling about Derek, he thought to himself that he was an aggressive person, and he took what he wanted from people. He could tell he wasn't a great lawyer, and that he would lie to a lot of people just to win and make money.

Frank and John became good friends over the next few months, hanging out at John's house to going out. They even took trips to different places they had never been before. Even though John was having a good time, he could still feel that emptiness that only his wife was able to fill. Frank was seeing a girl for a little while, and John felt like he was getting in the way. So he backed off a little, bit by bit, to let Frank spend time with his girlfriend. He told frank that even though he was having a great time, he needed to focus more on the business.

John's father was working on closing a huge business deal that would bring the company billions over the next twenty years and needed him to help him close it. So John told Frank that he would be working with his father for the next few months, flying to China and all over the world to meet up with new and old clients for business. John took his daughter with him so she wouldn't feel like her dad was too busy to be with her.

Even though he was working all day and most the night, they went out to a lot of places and saw just about everything they could see in different places over the world. He knew that his daughter was the only person he has left that meant the world to him, and the only thing that made him happy was to see her happy in life.

After they came back a few months later, John felt like his bond between him and Marri was stronger than ever. They talked about everything, she even asked if he would find another woman to be with.

John didn't know what to say, but he told her, "Nobody could come between us and how much I love you, but the thought of being alone for the rest of his life was kind on making him lonely.

As he was walking back to his office one day, he saw that they had hired a new woman, Michelle at tje front when he walks to his office. He was very attracted to her, she was very pretty and had a beautiful smile.

He introduced himself to her. He said hi, im your boss. One day, this company will be mine." He didnt know what else to say because he was so nervous.

She already knew who he was. "Do you want to get a drink one night after work?"

Scared, John said, "I will think about it. I'm still dealing with a loss, and I don't know if I'm ready."

A few weeks went by, and Michelle was still asking him out on a date. John told Frank about her, he asked what should I do.

Frank said, "Only go out with her if you feel like it's the right thing to do." Frank knew what John had been going through and how scared he was to start over with another person because of how close he was with his wife.

John was super nervous. He liked Michelle and knew she was a very nice women and was growing quickly in the company. He told her he will go out with her, but only if Frank and his girlfriend could go too. She said that fine, she was new the town and could use a few more friends to go out with.

CHAPTER 3

After a few dates with Michelle, John became increasingly open about letting her in his life. He started to tell her more and more about his life, his childhood, and Nicole.

He asked her, "Would you like to meet my six-year-old daughter for a fun night out at a pizza place that has games and rides?"

She said, "I would love to meet her. I'm so excited that you're taking the next step in our relationship." so the next day they planned for a fun night out.

Marri was a little scared at first, but after a few hours of playing games and eating pizza, she began to see how happy her dad was and wanted to give Michelle a chance to get to know her. John saw that his daughter was opening up to Michelle, and he felt that he was starting to live again. The next step was to introduce her to his parents. He knew how his father was and thought that his father wouldnt approve of her but when they meet they loved her.

John's father knew how much pain he was in when Nicole died. His father didnt like john making his own choices withou talking ti him first about it, he said "Make sure this is something you want in your life. Be careful because you are a rich young man, and most women just want money."

John told his father, "I will be careful. I am starting to feel happy again, and I really would like to be with someone who cared about me and made me feel loved again." After a dinner and laughing and talking,

he told Michelle that he wanted her to move in with him and take their relationship to another level. She was so happy that they would be spending more time together. The next day she told everyone at work how happy she was with John. He found himself being nicer to people at work, even going around to meet people and try to get to know them on a personal level.

Nobody had seen this side of John before, and they liked it. Work became fun for him, and he enjoyed waking up every morning to Michelle and Marri. Life was good again, he felt like nothing else matters. John would take Michelle out a lot and buy her all kinds of expensive stuff, like cars, clothes, or shoes. Whatever she wanted, he would give her.

She told him that she was in love with him and never felt like this before. John was happy because he had a beautiful woman in his life that loved him and his daughter and would love to be with him for the rest of her life. He felt that he could see them as husband and wife one day, and that scared him. He didn't ever want to go through what he endured with his wife ever again.

He told her, that he loved her too but he's not ready to get married at this time because I'm scared to lose you lile i lost Nicole.

She started to cry. "I understand. When you are ready to make the final step in our relationship, I would be right there waiting for you."

John felt a huge relief. He thought she would have left him if he didn't ask her to marry him.

They would get closer and closer over the next few months, spending more money and going even more places together. Marri had never seen her dad this happy before, even with her mom. John was in love again. He was so happy that he was able to find another woman that brought home so much joy in life. Frank and his girlfriend were coming around a lot too, and Derek was getting jealous that he was the only one without a girlfriend.

Derek started seeing how happy Frank was in his relationship and he didn't like it. One night, they went out to the bar, just the guys, for drinks to talk about what was going on with Derek and why he was being so jealous about John.

He told them, "It's just seeing you guys happy all the time. I want to feel the love that you guys feel.

John felt bad about how Derek was felling and he told him "I'm sorry for the way I've been toward you. I want us all to be friends. I'm going to ask Michelle to marry me, and I want the both of you up there with me when I get married."

Frank and Derek were super excited and honored that he would ask them to be up there, so they celebrated all night drinking and having a great time.

The next day, John took the day off and took Marri with him to go look at rings to buy Michelle. She was excited because she really liked to see her dad happy and she liked Michelle a lot. They went to an expensive jewelry store to pick out a ring. John saw one as soon as he stepped foot in the store. It was just calling his name. It was so beautiful and big that he didn't care how much it cost. He just knew that that one was the one.

The jeweler tried showing him different rings, but John knew that none of them would be like that one. After looking at the other rings he bought the onat that he first saw when he walked in. The ring had cost him a million dollars, and he was never that excited to spend so much money in his life.

Now it was finally hitting him that it was time to ask her to marry him, so he told her that they were going on a trip to Hawaii for the weekend. She was to meet him at the airport board on the families private plane.

He didn't want her to know, so he told her that it was a business trip and she would have to stay at the hotel with his daughter when they got there. He told Michelle that, I know that this is a business trip I still want you two to be there with me. She had never been there, so she started planning a lot of things for her and Marri to do while her father was out on business.

When they got there, John told her, "Go to the hotel. I'll meet up with you later."

She said, "We're going to have a girl's day. Just call me when you are done."

John wanted it to be perfect so he rented a yacht for the night and had a huge fireworks display set up for her in the middle of the ocean over looking all the hotels at night.

After she got back from spending the day with Marri, John was waiting for her in a suit. "I want to take you out to eat dinner."

She hurried up and got dressed with Marri in the clothes they bought earlier that day. John took them to a seafood restaurant that had an amazing view overlooking the ocean.

"I have a boat waiting for you and want to take you into the ocean to look at the island from a boat."

When they got on the boat, they had some drinks and danced to some music that he put on.

He told her, "I'm so in love with you. I know how much you love me." He got on one knee, reached into his pocket, and pulled out that beautiful ring. "Will you marry me?"

"Yes!"

And when she did, the fireworks went off. Both he and Marri were so happy. They all danced for the rest of the night. They had such an amazing night, John felt complete again, and he was excited to finally have a whole family again.

CHAPTER 4

That wedding was massive, and all of John's father's friends from all over the world were there. It was a perfect, beautiful ceremony and a fresh start to John's life. Marri was so happy to have a mother figure in her life again.

As a wedding gift to John, his father had all the proper paperwork done up to sign that would make John CEO of the company. He was amazed that his father was finally seeing him as the man he was and believing that he was responsible to run the business. He was now in charge of all overseas clients that he was trying so hard to close the deal for his dad and show him that he was ready.

John's life was now complete. All his hard work, late nights at the office, the blood and tears, and pain that he been through finally paid off. Michelle was so happy for her husband because now he could spend even more time at home with her. Now that John was the company owner, he made his wife as vice president. He asked Frank if he wanted a new position so he could help him make his company the best it had ever been.

Stunned, Frank knew he couldn't pass up an opportunity like this to make more money and to work with his best friend. Derek overheard John offering Frank the position, and he became mad. Derek knew that this position would take Frank away from him and Frank wouldn't want to hang out with him as much as he wanted to.

The wedding party continued all through the night with lots of drinking, dancing, laughing, and just having the best times of their lives. John was still in shock that this was all happening to him at this time in life, and at that moment, he missed Nicole and wished she could have been there to see him as the new owner of the company. He went outside to get some fresh air, and Frank followed after him.

Frank asked, "What's wrong? You just became one of the richest person in the world. Why are you not excited?"

"I am. I really wish Nicole could be here and see all the things I accomplished since she passed away."

Michelle happened to be walking outside and overheard him talking about Nicole and how much he missed her. She was mad but didn't say anything to John. She ran into the bathroom crying, but as she did that, Derek saw.

Derek waited until she came out. "What's wrong? Why are you crying? You're beautiful, and this is a day of celebration."

"I overheard John talking about how much he misses Nicole and wishes that she was here to see him take over his father's business."

"It's okay. John is just drunk, and he doesn't know how to treat a woman as pretty as you are. If you need anybody to talk to, don't hesitate to come find me."

"Okay."

He gave her his number. "Just in case you might need a lawyer in the near future."

When John came back inside from talking to Frank, he saw Michelle standing alone, away from everyone. "What's wrong?" he asked.

"Nothing. I just needed a few minutes away from everyone because there is a lot of people I don't know. I just wanted to be alone."

The night was coming to an end, and everybody started leaving and saying their good-byes. Everyone was pretty drunk, including John, by the end on the night. They took a limo back home, and Michelle had to help John into bed because he wasn't able to walk straight. She helped him take off his clothes and put him in bed.

John was so drunk that he was calling her Nicole. Michelle was very upset, so upset that she left him there, ran out the room, and got on the phone and called Derek.

"He keeps calling me Nicole. I know he's not fully over her."

"It's okay. You just need to write down and record anything like this, so if you take him to court, you will have a better chance of winning if it could prove him not being a good husband."

"I love John, but I don't want to be the shadow of another woman."

"You are a very beautiful woman, and you shouldn't be second to anyone."

"What should I do?" she asked.

"John is a very rich man. If something were to happen and you were to get a divorce, you would get a lot of money, along with the company since he made you the vice president."

"I couldn't do something like that to him. He is a good man and loving father to his daughter."

"That might be true, but think of all the money and freedom you will have when you are rich enough to be who you want to be and do what you want to do."

"I will think about it, and I will do what you ask in the time to come."

The next day, John woke up on the floor with a massive headache and didn't remember what happened. He thought to himself, *I hope I didn't do or say anything wrong. When I black out, I can't remember if I said or did anything to hurt anybody.*

"Michelle!" But he didn't hear anything at all.

He got up and got dressed, and he went downstairs to see where she could be. He found a note on the table saying, "I made u a fresh pot of coffee. I went to have lunch with a friend and will be home later."

He drank some coffee, trying to wake himself up so he could remember anything from last night after he came home.

Michelle decided she was going to meet up with Derek for lunch and talk more about how she could get a lot of money if she decided to get a divorce from John. John had no idea that his wife was out with Derek for lunch, plotting on how she could take everything away from him.

CHAPTER 5

While at lunch with Derek, Michelle was really interested in what Derek was telling her about how to get John for all his money and take him for everything he had.

He told her, "The only way to get him is to make it look like he's cheating with another girl. Make it look like he's an abusive and violent person." He continued, "I'm falling for you. You should be with a man who would really take of you and love you like you should be loved."

Michelle said, "I'm falling for you too. I always thought you were a good-looking man."

They decided to come up with a plan to set up John so it would look like he was an abusive and violent person. He would not have a chance in a courtroom.

"I know a friend who knows some hookers. I could make it look like John met her at a nightclub. I could put something in his drink so he wouldn't remember anything that happened, but he would see what he did the next day. You will have to get into an argument in front of people so you would have witnesses who would stand up for you in court. Someone would have to hit you in the face to make it look like John was the one who beat you. Then we would have to get video or pictures on John with the hookers in bed and to get her to testify against John, saying they had sex together."

Michelle was kind of nervous, but she agreed to pay Derek to help her get John for everything he had. "I will pay you a million dollars if you would guarantee that I would get away with setting John up."

"It would be fast and easy. To the jury, John would definitely be guilty, and he would have no choice but to settle for whatever she was suing him for."

"I want to take him for all his money and his company that his dad gave him. I don't want him to have anything but his daughter left. I don't want him to be without her because he is a good father and he does love Marri with all his heart.

"When the courts are done with him he will have nothing but the clothes on his back, his daughter, and a few things, but nothing worth of value."

After they had lunch, Derek kissed Michelle. "I will be there to walk you through the steps of what you have to do next."

She left Derek, got in her car, and checked her phone. She had ten missed calls from John. She called him back.

"My phone has been acting up these last few days. I'm done having lunch with my friend."

John told her, "I'm sorry for the way I was acting, and I apologize if I did anything stupid last night. I can't remember much."

"You were really drunk and yelling at me a lot. That's why I left, to give you some time alone to think of what you did."

John felt horrible because he knew he was not that type of person to get violent or argue with his wife. He wanted to surprise her with a huge bear and flowers for when she got back to show her that he was sorry and he loved her very much.

When she arrived back at home, there was a ten-foot teddy bear with two trucks full of roses in the driveway. She was amazed that he did that for her, but in her head, she still wanted to get him for everything.

John told her, "I'm so sorry for my behavior. I will never get upset or show any type of anger toward you ever again."

"It's okay. I forgive you for what you did. I love you and will never leave you."

John wanted to take her to an expensive restaurant for dinner and drinks to whatever place she wanted to go. That night, they went to the most expensive Italian restaurant that they could find. John bought the most expensive bottle of wine for Michelle because she loved wine.

The whole time they were there, Derek had been texting her, telling her that he missed and loved her. He said he got the hookers who were going to be with John. He also told her that it was coming closer for them to be ready to go along with the plan.

He texted her, "We should do it by the weekend."

Later in the dinner, John got a text from Frank saying that Derek wanted to celebrate a win he got in court he has been working on for months. He wanted to go out to the club this weekend and said that he and Michelle should go.

John asked Michelle, "Do you want to go out with me and the boys this weekend to celebrate a win that Derek got in court?"

"Yes! I would love to go out with you. I will have a great time with everyone."

Michelle knew the plan was going down this weekend. She got a text from Derek, asking if she had video cameras in the house. And if so, she would have to make sure that the camera would make the video they needed to use for court.

Derek was ready to set John up and all he needed was to set up some hidden cameras in the house and it would be done. I will make sure that there will be one in the bedroom, and in the bathroom. Or I will be able to take pictures when the time comes. You can tell the court that u set them up because you knew he was cheating on you and you had to make sure he was.

During the rest of the week, she didn't want John to think she was up to something, so she acted like nothing was wrong and going on with her day to day things.

It was time to go out and hit the club, so John got dressed up really nice, and so did Michelle.

"I'm not going to drink," he promised her. You won't have a problem with me not remembering anything because I'm done with drinking.

When they get there, Frank and his girlfriend as well as Derek were there, waiting in the front of the club for them. They got in and started dancing and having a good time.

Derek asked John, "Why aren't you drinking?"

"I don't want to do anything stupid. The last time I got drunk, I blacked out and didn't remember anything."

"This is a celebration. You have to have at least one drink with me."

John said, "Fine. Just one drink, but that's it.

Derek bought him one drink, and when he brought it, he dropped in some drugs so John would not be able to remember anything. Derek saw Michelle from across the room and gave her the sign that it was in his drink and it will be working soon after he drinks it.

Michelle walked up to John and saw he had a drink in his hands. "What are you doing?"

John said, "It's only one drink. I will be fine. That's the only one I will have for the night."

She somewhat got mad and walked off. John tried to follow her, but Derek pulled him back. "Finish the drink with me."

John hurried up and drank the beverage so he could go after Michelle. And when he caught up with her, she started yelling at him, making it look like an argument, like Derek wanted. John was trying to calm her down, saying it was only one drink, but she wasn't having it.

A few minutes later, John began to feel really drunk. He couldn't walk straight. Michelle kept the arguing with him to the point where he began to argue back, and now everyone could see them fighting in the club. He was telling her that he hated her and wished she were dead. Now John had no clue what was going on, and everybody could see how drunk he was.

Frank noticed that John was drunk, and he decided to help him get into the limo and go home. Michelle told Frank and Derek that she was going to make sure that John got home okay. So they left. Derek told Frank that he was going to stay at the club for a bit to keep partying. Frank said that he and his girlfriend were going home.

Michelle called Derek and told him that he was knocked out in the limo. "Hurry quick!"

Derek raced over to the house after he picked up the hooker. He told Michelle, "Make sure the camera is on in the house."

And she did. They made it look like Michelle dropped him off at home and the hookers came into the house after Michelle left. The hooker got into bed with John, took off his clothes, and started taking pictures of the both of them together and got on top of him to make it look to the camera that they were having sex.

Derek was telling Michelle that she had to make it look like John hit her, so she hit herself a few times in the face to make it look like he hit her in the limo. That was why she dropped him off at home and left. When she came home to make it look like she was coming to get her stuff to leave him, she saw that he was in bed with another woman. Everything was going as planned, and nobody would be able to believe him

John had no idea that this was happening, but she now had all the evidence she needed to frame him and get him for everything he had.

CHAPTER 6

The next morning, John woke up to Michelle yelling at him and asking him why there was a woman in the bed with him. He was very confused on what was going on. He was extremely hungover and couldn't remember anything. John saw that there was another woman, but he had no clue who she was, lying naked with him in the bed.

"I went to the club and only had one drink. I don't remember anything else. I have no clue how I got home or how this woman got in the house and bed with me."

Angry, Michelle told him, "I want a divorce. I'm going to make sure you pay for everything you have put me through."

John was begging her not to leave. "I really only had one drink. I'm sorry! Please stay."

She started to pack her bags. "My lawyer will get in contact with you. I will be back to get my things Don't try to get a hold of me."

John started crying because he had no idea what went on last night and he didn't know what would happen now because of what occurred.

Michelle left and took some stuff and went to her parents' house to stay there until everything got figured out about what would happen to John.

Right after she left, John called Derek and told him what happened. "I will need you when the time comes to represent me in court as my lawyer."

Derek said, "I'm already working on a case. I couldn't take on another one at this time. But I will set you up with a good friend in the firm I work for. He's a really good lawyer in what you are dealing with."

"Okay. Give him my number so I could get him to help me as soon as possible."

John was still feeling whatever was in his system, so he decided to lay down and try to sleep it off for a while. He wanted to have a strong mind and rested body so he could figure out what was going to happen to him if he went to court.

Later that night, he woke up to a bunch of missed calls and voice messages from Frank, asking him what was going on and why he hadn't called back because he hadn't heard from him since he left the club.

John called him back and told him what happened with everything that he could remember. "Michelle left me. She said she wants a divorce."

Frank was stunned. "I only saw you with one drink. I can't understand how you could get so drunk and not remember anything."

"It's happened before. I drank and didn't remember anything, but I had way more drinks."

"If you went to court, she could try to take everything from you. You need to figure something out fast before you lose everything."

"Derek recommended a lawyer because he's too busy now to take on another case."

After getting off the phone with Frank, John called the lawyer and talked to him, asking if he could take on a case if it went to court.

"Yes, but it would be a tough case. We would have to prove that she did something wrong. I can't see that she has done anything wrong at the time."

"I'll keep in touch with you. I really want you to help me win the case."

The next day, John woke up to a knock on the door. It was a man in a suit, holding papers saying that he was to be in court for divorce proceedings next week. John was hurt because he knew he must have done something so bad that his wife would take him to court and file for divorce.

John called his dad and asked for some help.

His dad didn't want to talk to him. "How could you do something like that to put your company and reputation at risk?"

John was pissed that his father would only care about what would happen to the company and his name if he would lose everything that his dad gave him.

So the time came to appear for the first court hearing. John showed up with the lawyer that Derek had recommended to him. John sat down first, waiting for Michelle to arrive. John was scared because he had no idea of what would happen to him, but he knew he would be good because he had an excellent lawyer.

Then Michelle walked in. Derek was right behind her.

John looked at him. "What's going on? Why are you with her?"

"I am representing Michelle, and I cannot speak to you about anything."

John knew at this point that Derek betrayed him. He thought that Derek was his friend, and he couldn't believe what he was seeing. Why *would he do something like this to me? What did I ever do to him for him to do this to me?*

They started the trial, and John was at a loss for words. Michelle went to the bench first. Derek was asking her how their relationship was and how they met. He inquired about them dating before they got married.

"We met at work. Everything was great at first, but when he would start drinking, he would be a whole different person. He would black out and be a very violent person, often hitting me." She even showed the jury her bruises on her ribs and the black eye he gave her.

John was shocked because she was up there lying to everyone. He would have never put his hands on her, not one time. He might have gotten mad a few times and yelled, but he never ever put his hands on her.

Michelle would go on to say she had been unhappy for a very long time because he couldn't get over his wife, Nicole. She talked about how she had passed away from cancer. He would always talk about her and never give me the love that I deserved.

When she was done telling lies about John, it was his turn to get up there. He didn't know what to say after she was up there, telling stories to make herself look good. His lawyer asked him how they met and how their relationship was.

"Our relationship was great. I had never put my hands on her. She's a liar!" But the way he said it made him look like he had anger problems.

John was very upset that she said the stuff she did, and it wasn't making his case look too good in his favor. His lawyer asked him questions about his drinking and anger. It was like he was working with Derek and not him. John felt set up, like he didn't have a chance to win.

The end of the first court day was over, and John just wanted to give up. The next day, John told himself that he would go in there, tell his story, and hope that he could come out with a win.

Michelle's next witness was the hooker she hired to set up John. She would go on the tell the jury that she and John had been together a few times and said he would pay her to do sexual acts for money.

John stood up and started yelling, "She's a liar!"

His anger was getting him into so much trouble with the jury and judge.

The judge told him, "Sir, your next outburst will result in you going to jail if you cannot control yourself."

So John let her finish. She would go on telling them that she went home with him on the night they went out. John was very drunk, and he gave her money to beat her and have rough sex with her.

At this time, John was so upset that he knew he had no chance to win. John called his only witness, Frank.

Frank told the judge, "John is a great, loving man, caring to all his friends and family. He is a great father and doesn't know why this is going on with him. John cares about other people more than he cares about himself. He put his daughter over everyone else." Frank had nothing but great things to say about his friend, John. "Derek was there with us at the bar drinking, and he knows more than what he is telling us."

Derek would go on to say, "John is a huge drinker, and that night, I was telling him not to drink too much. John told me that he was a grown man who was rich and could do whatever he wanted."

John could not believe what was going on. He was so mad that this was happening to him.

The second day of court was coming to an end, and the third day would be the final day. John knew he was in trouble and Michelle would try to get everything she could from him.

The judge came to a decision, and it was in favor of Michelle.

The judge was upset with John. "People like you make this world a bad place. Just because you have money, you think you can hit and cheat on people who can't do anything to defend themselves."

She rewarded Michelle everything she was asking for—the house, the company, and most of John's cars and other properties he owned. That meant John would be left with next to nothing. Just like that, everything he had worked for his whole life was gone. He felt so upset and betrayed. He didn't know what to do or where to go.

When he walked out of the courtroom, there were TV cameras and reporters everywhere asking him why would he beat her, how did it feel to lose everything, and how did it feel to be like everyone else who had no money. John knew that he had some backup money. It wasn't much, but he would have to figure out his next move for him and his daughter.

CHAPTER 7

Michelle spent no time making sure that John would be out on the streets. But the next day, all kinds of movers were there, taking out all of his stuff. She donated and sold whatever she didn't like. The only things she let him have were some clothes.

John was hurt. Once again he felt like not living. Nobody wouls ever believe him that he disnt do it. He took his and Marri's clothes and packed them into the only car she let him have and drove off. He called Frank's and asked to stay at his house for a few weeks until he could find a job and a place to go. Frank was the only true friend he had, and he knew he could count on him.

But Frank's house wasn't big, and his landlord told him that he couldn't have extra people living with him. Frank told him he could stay, but he woild have to not get caught at his hoise or we coild get kicked out. John knew he didn't have much time there, so he would have to look for work fast.

When he got to Frank's house, Frank hugged him. "This will be over soon. You have nothing to worry about. You will get back on your feet real quick.

John starting crying, but he didn't want his daughter to see him bawl. He told her that he had something in his eyes and that why they were watering. Frank could tell that John was destroyed inside because he never had seen him cry before. John had always been a strong man because of how his father would be so rough with him and never show him any type of love. Frank decided to make John and Marri a nice home-cooked meal, and he even offered him a drink.

But John turned it down. "I am never going to drink again. Every time I drink, something bad happens."

So after dinner and a long talk with Frank about how he was going to make the best of his situation, John told Frank that he was still going to be the best dad to his daughter as he could be.

Frank showed John to where he would be sleeping. "You'll have to find a different place to live soon because of my landlord."

John told Frank, "I can't thank you enough for what you are doing for Marri and me. When I get back on my feet, I will take care of you."

"I don't want anything from you, just that we be friends for life."

The next day, John felt confident that he would find a job quickly because of who he was, so he got up and starting job hunting. John had no idea that Michelle went to the news, telling them how he would beat her. She said he was an alcoholic and such a bad person to her and other people. She promised John before he left that she was going to destroy his life and he would never be able to work in the city again.

John went to every big company in the city, putting in applications and résumés, hoping that someone would call him for an interview. But nobody did. He was all over the news, and people were talking about him, saying they worked for him and all he cared about was money and his business and never about the people who worked for him.

A few days went by, and still there were no calls. But he wasn't going to give up. He starting putting in applications at places he would never think about putting them in before. He went to restaurants, grocery stores, and gas stations, just about anywhere that he could make some type of money. But John was a very known person around town, and from what the news was saying about him, he was a woman beater and alcoholic. So nobody would hire him.

John knew that the only money he had was being spent quickly because he had to make sure that his daughter had something to eat and had clothes on her back. After a long day of looking for work, John decided to take a trip to his parents' house with Marri and see if he could get some money from his dad.

When he got there, his dad was very upset with him. He didn't ever want to let John or Marri in his house, but his mom did. John was trying to explain that he was set up, but he couldn't prove it to anybody because nobody would listen to him.

John's father didn't care about what he had to say. All he cared about was how he ruined his name and how disappointed he was in him for letting someone come into his life and just take everything he worked so hard for.

John told his father, "I had no idea that she and my lawyer friend would have set me up like that to take all my money and everything else I had."

His father still didn't care about what he said. "It's time to leave. I don't want to speak to you again."

Sad, John started to get angry. "I'm broke, and I need your help for the first time in my life. It's hard to ask you for help, but I really need it."

"No. I will never help you out. I don't have a son anymore."

As John was walking out of the house, he looked at his mom. "How can you let him just throw us out and not say anything?"

His mother looked up at his dad.

"Do not say anything to him, and go back in the kitchen."

John looked at Marri. "Say good-bye because this will be the last time you see your grandpa and grandma."

John got in his car and drove clear across town to Frank's house, saying nothing to his daughter because he was so hurt inside. The whole time, he was just thinking of how his father was never there for him, and all he wanted was his father to be proud of what he accomplished in life. He felt so crushed that his own family would turn their backs on him and his daughter.

When he got back to Frank's, Frank told him, "My landlord knows you have been staying there and said I could only let you stay one more night before you would have to leave."

John understood. "Thank you for risking getting kicked out so my daughter and I could have a place to go for a while. I have some money, and I will try to find a weekly place that I could pay for a few weeks and worry about finding a job or some kind of work."

So John found a place he could stay at. It was in a bad neighborhood, but it was cheap. He paid for a month's stay, hoping that was all he would need to stay there before he would have a bigger place and a job before his time was up. He barely had any clothes for him and Marri, and he didn't have a lot of money left for food, but he knew he would make it work.

John still stayed in contact with Frank and would let him know that he was doing okay. Frank would tell him that everything would be fine. Frank told John to let him know if he needed anything like food or money. He would do his best, but Frank also didn't have a job because both had lost their jobs to Michelle.

John still had to find a job fast, but he didn't have anyone to watch his daughter while he went out job hunting. He would have to leave her at the place sometimes so he could find a job.

A few more weeks went by, and there were still no calls from anywhere he applied for. Now he was starting to worry because his money was running low and all he had left to sell was his car. Another week went by, and he decided to put his car up for sale to see what he could get for it. John was really stressed out because he knew he had nobody who could help him out, but he knew he must continue to be strong for his daughter.

One day when he came back from looking for work, he saw a man at his door, saying he wanted to buy his car. It was the first person to respond to his ad in the paper. John was asking $10,000 for his car, and the guy offered him half. John knew it was a horrible offer, but he didn't have any money left. So after a long talk with the guy, trying to at least get some more money, he finally talked him into $6,500 for it.

He was happy about that and knew the money would get him just a little further than he was. He saw in the paper that they were hiring people at a construction company that wasn't too far from where he was staying at. He got on the bus with Marri and went down there.

When he got there, he saw a long line of people there, also looking for a job. He waited for three hours until he finally got to see a hiring manager.

He told the guy who he was. "I'm down and out and need a job. I will take whatever you have left."

The manager said, "All I have left is a part-time position that pays only eight dollars an hour."

John said, "I will take it!"

But the manager told him, "It's not a permanent position, and I don't know if it will be open long."

John didn't care. He was just happy that he had a job, and it had been so long since he worked. John left the construction company in a whole new better mood because things were getting better for him.

CHAPTER 8

The next Monday, John started his new job. It was only three days a week, and it wasn't much, but he was happy to have a job. John would have to get up by three in the morning to get ready for work, but the only thing that worried him the most was that he would have to leave his daughter at the apartment for six hours on the days he worked. School was starting in a few months, so he wouldn't have to leave her at home for too much longer before she would be in school.

John was really liking his job. His coworkers didn't really care too much about him because of who he was. John just stayed away from them and got his job done the best way he could. The guys at work would call him a wife beater and a rich kid and said he deserved what happened to him.

John tried to explain to them what happened and said he wasn't who they thought he was, but they didn't listen to him. Word got back to the bosses that some workers didn't like John and they had planned to beat him up one day after work.

The next day, John's boss pulled him in the office and let John know that, even though he was a good worker, his time and services were no longer needed because of the things that were going on in the workplace.

Upset, John told his boss, "I really need this job because I haven't been able to get another job anywhere else because of who I am."

"I'm very sorry, but it is out of my hands. If you stayed, the other workers would hurt you. I don't want that to happen to you." He paid John for the time he was there and told him to good luck.

John gathered his things and left without saying anything. When he got back to his apartment, he told Marri what happened.

"I will find another job soon, but I have enough money for us to live off of for a few more months."

The next day, he went to the grocery store to get some food and the paper to find more jobs. He saw that a dishwasher job had opened at a restaurant just around the corner from his place.

The next day, he got on the bus and went down to get the job. When he got there, he talked to someone who told him the job was nights but only four hours a day.

"It's fine. I could do it."

The job didn't pay much, but it was one that he needed.

"You need to buy some black, slick-resistant shoes and black pants."

"No problem. I can start right away."

A few weeks went by with this job, and John was dealing with the same issues as the construction company. Everyone there didn't like him for who he was and what he did to his ex-wife. He tried not to let it get to him, but it just seemed like, wherever he would go, people would not give him a chance to explain himself and let him tell his side of the story.

Everyone was judging John, and no one knew what kind of man he was. He didn't understand why people could be so judgmental and why they couldn't just give him a chance to show that he was a good man, just having a bad time in his life.

That same day when he was at work, he was let go because they told him he just wasn't working out for the position he had. John went back home this time with his head down, feeling like he could not get a break. His money was running out, and he would only have enough money to get him to the end of the month. Then he would be broke for good.

He found a place that could pay daily for his time, but a lot of people would do it too. So it was so hard to get in. He went down there a few times during the week, but he was unable to get any work because there was just not enough work for everyone who was out of work. John noticed the people who were trying to get a job looked like they were a bunch of homeless people.

He decided to ask a few guys how they got by and what else they would do for money and food.

One guy told him, "I will just find a place, stand on the corner, and ask people for money. But that's hard because of a lot of people will be doing that too."

Another guy said, "Once a week, there's a potluck at a church, and they will give food and sometimes clothes when they have any."

John replied, "I've never been in this situation, and I could use all the advice I could get."

The guys also told him about a shelter that was up the road a ways, but it was hard to get into because it was usually full. They had been on the streets a long time. They told him that it had been rough, but they had gotten used to it.

John told them, "Thank you for your help. It's nice talking to someone who doesn't judge me for who I am."

John really needed a break soon, or he knew it wouldn't be long before he would have nowhere to go and would be out on the streets with his daughter. John was so lost. His money was just about out, and he had no motivation left to move forward. He tried just about everything he could do to be a good man and a great father. He just needed some help that he couldn't get from anyone. He wanted to just give up on life. He had never been this broke in his whole life. He always had his father to help him and give him money if he needed it. For the first time in his life, he had no help and couldn't call on anyone for assistance.

CHAPTER 9

It came time for John and Marri to be out on the streets. He had no job and no money, and he barely had any food left for the both of them. He decided to try to go to the shelter to see if they had some beds they could sleep on for the night or longer if needed.

The shelter was across town, so he had no money for the bus. They had a long way to walk with all their stuff.

As they started walking, Marri was asking her dad, "Are things going to get better for us? Why is this happening to us and not someone else?"

John told her, "Bad things happened to good people all the time, but it would get better for us soon. I promise it will. I am going to make sure we will have everything we need to survive. I will never leave you, and one day, we will have everything we once had but better."

"I don't want all the fancy things we once had. All I want is to be with you and not be alone."

"I promise you that I will never leave you alone by yourself. We will have a big house together, and it will be just us."

By the time they got to the shelter, they had some great conversations about life and how they would get through the situation they were in. He saw that there was a long line from the front door to around the building. He had no choice but to wait in line to see if they would have enough room for them to get a bed. John felt so hurt that this was happening to him and Marri. He thought it was his fault they were having such a hard time. He started to cry, but he didn't want Marri to see him.

She looked up at him. "Why are you crying?"

"I'm not. It's windy outside, and I got something in my eyes." He was trying to stay positive and not let her see him falling apart.

They stood outside for hours, and John noticed a lot of homeless people were out on the streets. He wondered why their own government wasn't doing anything to help out people who really needed it, like him.

He asked a few people, "Why is the line so long? Why do we have to wait so long to get a bed?"

One person told him, "This is the only shelter in town that will help people. On Saturdays, a group from the local church comes to hand out food for us."

John asked the man, "Why doesn't the government have more programs that will help homeless people get back on their feet or have something that could help them get their GEDs or find jobs so they could get off the streets one day?"

The man replied, "I've never heard of a program like that. I am just thankful that we get to come here on Saturdays to get a warm meal and maybe a blanket if it gets too cold when we are out on the streets."

John was angry by the end of their conversation that barely any kind of program helped homeless people at all. He was thinking to himself, *If I would have known about this when I had the money, I would have done more things for people who didn't have anything and who really needed it.*

John felt good at that moment that he was able to talk to some people who had been through the struggle and were still going through it. They talked for hours just about life and how hard it had been for him and his daughter. The man told him about his life. He said how he had been on the streets for years and how people would treat him like he was nothing and would spit and kick him.

They would yell at him, "Try getting a real job" and "Stop asking people for help." He too had been to hell and back, but he didn't give up and just thanked the Lord that he was still alive.

John didn't know about God so he couldn't tell him about how thankful he was. John just told the man, "I'm just trying to survive on the streets with my daughter. I was once rich and had it all, but I lost everything to my ex-wife, who I knew set me up to take all my money."

By the time they got up to the door, a guy came out and told everyone that they had no more room and they would have to come back tomorrow at eight in the morning to wait to get a bed. John was disappointed.

He looked down at Marri. "It will be okay. We will find a place to go to soon."

John went up to the man. "I'm out here on the streets with my daughter. Is there anything I could do to help?" John had tears in his eyes because he knew how hard it was to ask someone for help.

The man saw that John was about to cry and he was with his daughter. He told John to wait right there because he knew there wasn't a bed left, but maybe he could give John something to help him while he was out on the streets.

Ten minutes went by, and the door opened. The man came back with two blankets, a loaf of bread, a Bible, and twenty bucks.

"This is all I could get you. I will pray for you and your daughter. God will help you through your journey in life."

John told the man, "Thank you for all your help. I will try to get to the shelter earlier so we would have a bed to sleep on." John looked down at Marri. "I see a park and a store down the street. I'm going to use the money to get us some food that will last a few days. We're going to have to sleep at the park for the night." John rolled up their blankets and started walking in the direction of the store to get some food.

Marri asked her father on the way to the store, "Do you think we will be okay?"

"Yes. Do not worry. We are going through a rough time in life right now, but I know it will get better."

"How do you know?"

"I just have a strong feeling that we will be."

When they got to the store, he bought enough food to last about three days and sufficient water for a week. He just knew he would have to keep all the food and water close to him so nobody would try to take it from him. When they got to the park, John found a nice spot that looked like nobody who was homeless had been there for a while. It was out of sight from the traffic and eyes.

John knew that, if he were to get caught for anything, they would take his daughter from him, and his life would be over if that happened. John knew he couldn't stay at that spot for long, but it would have to do for now until he could find somewhere more permanent for him and Marri.

CHAPTER 10

His first night on the streets wasn't that bad for the both of them, it was a bit scary at first because he never lived on the streets. John made sure that his daughter was safe and she got to sleep through the whole night with no problems from other people. He knew the food that he had for the both of them would run out quickly and he had to make some kind of money or they would be hungry. He decided he was going to hit the street corners and ask for money or food, and hopefully some work. He went back to the store from the day before and found some cardboard. He ripped up of cardboard but needed a marker to write on it with.

He stood outside the store and asked people for a marker or pen. Finally a nice lady bought him a marker from inside the store and a bottle of water. He wrote on the cardboard, "Homeless and hungry. Please, anything will help. Thank you."

He went back to the park where he left Marri. "I'm going to have you stay here for a few hours so I could try to get some money."

He didn't have much time to ask people for help because they would have to stand back in line if they wanted a bed at the shelter. He decided to stay out there for only a few hours and then go stand in line at the shelter, hoping the line wasn't too long.

John had never done anything like this before so he didn't know what to expect. He just knew that he was to do whatever he had to do to make sure that Marri had clothes and food. He felt scared because he would have to stand out there for hours at a time, hoping that someone would stop and give him money or food. He would have to face his fear, get out there, and try to do his best for his daughter. He didn't care if he ate or had clothes. He just cared about her.

So he swallowed his pride and stood on the corner, holding his sign. A lot of people would just pass by not saying anything or even reading his sign. About an hour out there, an old lady rolled down her window, holding a ten-dollar bill.

When he got up to her window, she told him, "God bless. Please get some food."

"Thank you. I will definitely get food with it."

Another person had some change that was in her car and told him, "God bless."

A few more people would give him some money as well and tell him "God bless." John started to think about what they were telling him. It seemed to him that this God person wasn't so bad if everyone were telling him "God bless." He thought to himself, *Maybe I should open the Bible that they gave me at the shelter and see what it's all about.*

Another hour passed by, and John had over $100 in bills and change. He was so thankful that people were kind enough to give him money that he needed so bad to get him through his rough times. Standing outside most the day made John smell bad, and he knew, if he stunk, then so did Marri. And he would have to find a place fast to take a shower. He had to leave the corner because it was time to go back and stand in the line for the shelter.

He went back to Marri, whom he was so worried about, and showed her all the money he had made in a few hours. She was excited to see her dad so excited about something because it had been a long time since she saw him smile. He packed up their stuff and went to the shelter to stand in line.

When they got there, the line was long, but not as long as the day before. This time, he had more stuff to carry. He started to talk to a lady who was in line, and she was telling him what a beautiful daughter he had.

"Thank you. She's all I have." John told her about Nicole dying from cancer and the whole story on how he got to where he was.

She was sad. "Do not worry. God has a plan for you, and you will be back on your feet in no time."

Then it was time for them to get a bed. They were so happy that they would get to sleep in a bed. When they got inside, John saw the man who helped them the other day and went up to him to tell him thank you for all his help.

John introduced him to Marri. "The money you gave me saved us from going hungry for a few days."

The man started to tear up. "I got a strange feeling in his body to help you out." The man also gave him some soap and a towel and showed him where the showers were. "The hot water is limited, and there probably isn't any left."

"No problem. I just want to take a shower and be clean."

John went into the shower first and was really quick about it because Marri was waiting out there with all their stuff. He didn't take long, but he told Marri that it was so nice to take a shower. She got in, and John saw that she didn't have any clean clothes left. When she got done with her shower, he told her that he was going to take her to a store to get some clothes so she wouldn't have to keep wearing the same stuff throughout the week.

After they took their showers, he found the beds that were for them. He put all his stuff under his bed. "Marri, we made it through another day, and we need to be thankful for that."

As they laid there tired from the day, John looked around and saw a lot of people were in there, and they really needed help just as much as they did. He laid there thinking about the Bible and knew that he wanted to read it, but he also wanted Marri to read it as well. He wanted to see who God was, what he was doing for people, and how he was doing it.

He just stayed up as long as he could, thinking. Then finally he looked over and saw that Marri was sleeping. Then he fell asleep too.

The next day, he woke up feeling good because he got some great sleep and so did Marri. He got up out of his bed, looked down, and saw that all of his stuff was gone. Someone took his and Marri's stuff while they were sleeping.

John was angry, yelling at everyone, "Who took my stuff?"

Nobody answered him. He just kept on yelling until someone came up to him and told him that he would have to take the rest of his stuff and leave and never come back. The only thing they left was his Bible and some clothes. They took his water and all his food.

John was right back to where he started before. At least he still had the money he got from asking people on the street the day before. He packed up what was left and left to go look for a new place to go. He felt so down because, once things started looking up, they just went bad again. He was back to the point of giving up again.

They walked for hours and hours and stumbled into a neighborhood that wasn't in the best of places, but he saw a house that had been abandoned and had a for-sale sign on it. The house looked like nobody had been there or tried fixing it up for years, so he decided to write down the address just in case he would be in trouble with the cops. He could tell them that he was living there so it looked like he wasn't homeless.

Down that same street were some apartment complexes, and in front of that was an empty dirt lot with a bunch of trees and bushes. He was thinking that this would be a perfect stop for both of them and nobody would even know they would be there because you couldn't see anything from the streets. An individual could barely see inside the dirt lot. It was perfect. There was a store across the street, a few fast-food places, and a couple restaurants where he could try to get a job at. He could stand on the corner and ask for help because it was by a major street that went from one side of town to the other, just on one street.

The place he just found made up for the bad day he was having. Throughout the rest of the day and night, he would break down trees and build a nice place that the rain and other types of weather couldn't get through.

He looked down at Marri and told her, "Now things are starting to look good in our direction."

He built a little path that only they knew was there, and only they could get to their place. For the first time in a while, John was happy because he knew good things would come from this.

CHAPTER 11

The next day, John wanted to make his new place more livable, so he went to a nearby store that sold household items and food goods. He bought more food and things they could use, like if it were a house that he just bought. John was feeling better that he had a place to call home for the time being until he actually was able to get a house for them.

Later that day, he and Marri walked around their new neighborhood, looking for places to eat at and schools to attend because she was going to have to start school soon. They found an elementary school that was really nice, and Marri was excited because she saw a lot of fun things to do there. John wanted the best for his daughter so he would sign her up within the next week because school was starting soon. He also wanted to see what kind of fast food or any kind of stores were around so he could find a job.

A convenience store was right across the street from where they were staying so it could be easy for them to get water and small snacks if they needed to. He would have to figure out how they were going to use the bathroom and take showers whenever they could.

Marri was running out of clothes so John promised he would take her to a thrift store the next day to find some clothes and shoes so she would have new stuff for school. She was so excited that she and her dad were going to be spending time together. John was a busy man with work in the past and didn't really spend too much time with his daughter, but he was realizing that.

When they got back to their spot from a long day of looking and getting new stuff for their place, John made Marri something to eat.

She asked, "Could you read me a bedtime story? You've never done that for me."

He felt sad that he never read her anything to her because he was so busy trying to please his father and make his father's company better at the time. Then he realized that his father never read him a bedtime story either. He told her that he would, but he didn't have a book. Then he remembered that he had the Bible that the guy had given him at the shelter.

He took it out, but he said, "I want us both to read it because I think we both should find out about what this Bible is about."

He opened it up and began to read to her. He read and read and read until he looked down to find Marri fast asleep. He told himself, *Wow, that was really good*. He wanted to read more, but he didn't want to read it without Marri, so he marked his place in the Bible and decided to lay down for the night.

The next day, they woke up with a lot of energy and love. John asked Marri, "Do you feel better today?"

"Yes, I do, Dad. Let's get up and make the best out of this day."

He made her something to eat, and then they both got dressed and started to walk to the thrift store to get her some clothes. John didn't have a lot of money left over so he knew he couldn't get her much right now, but he could get her enough to get by until he could afford more. He got her a few outfits and a pair of shoes to start off the new school year with.

After they left the thrift store, he told her that they were going to stop by the school to sign her up for the new school year. She was jumping up and down. She had never been to a public school and wanted to meet new friends, play, and be happy.

When he got there to sign her up, he was talking to someone there, and she told him that they needed her birth certificate and address of where there were staying at. John remembered that he had written down the address of that abandoned house, so he gave her that and told her that they just moved there from another house on the other side of town. He didn't want to tell her everything that happened, but he made it look like they had lost the house to a fire, along with his important paperwork and other stuff.

"That's okay. But it's important that you bring the proper paperwork that the school needs, like shot records."

He told her that he would have it by the first day of school, which was next week. He needed to find some type of work so he could have some kind of money for his family.

John found himself lonely a lot. He could only talk to Marri about certain things. So he decided to go to the store and get a journal to help. He could write down everything that had happened to him and stuff in the future. During the days, he wanted to write in his journal and at nights read the Bible to Marri. She was fascinated about the Bible just as much as he was. He wrote mostly the whole day in his journal about how he had everything and lost it to his ex-wife, how they became homeless, and all the struggles along the way.

He needed money so he walked around the neighborhood, looking for work. He put in a lot of applications and talked to a few managers about the positions that were posted on the buildings that he went to. People still recognized who he was, so most of the places told him no and even talked down on him.

It was starting to get hotter outside so he would have to drink more water during the days to come. He saw a man standing on one of the corners in the street with a sign, and he wanted to talk to him to see how else he could make some money or if he knew of any places where he could make daily money.

The man told him, "There's a day labor place up the road where you could get some work if you wanted to do construction or other types of trades. What are you good at doing?"

"Anything that involves making money to support my family."

He needed to make some money fast, so he went back to his place, grabbed his sign, and went back to the corner to ask people for help. He stood out there for a few hours and got some money, but it was enough to feed Marri, but not him. He saw a very expensive car get closer to him. He thought to himself, *This could be the one person who could help me out a lot if he gives me a lot of money.*

When the car got closer, John noticed that at one time in his life, when life was good, he had a car just like that one. Then the car was right next to him, and John looked.

"I had this same type of car and color."

It was his car, and when he looked closer, Michelle was in the passenger seat, and Derek was driving. He became so mad that he couldn't move from all the anger he had in him. He had been through so much because of those two people who wanted to destroy him and take all his money. He just kept looking at her, and she looked at his sign that he was holding.

She finally looked up at him and saw it was her ex-husband holding the sign, asking for help. She started to roll down the window to make sure it was him. When she knew it was him for sure, she rolled the window back up, and the car started to continue around the corner.

John was so mad that he was crying, and he ripped his sign in half and didn't notice he did that. He wanted do something to them so bad that he would have probably gone to jail for a long time. Then he started to think about Marri and where she would be if she didn't have her dad. He felt so depressed and sad that this was happening to him and Marri, and Michelle got to drive around in his car that he bought with his own money. She was living a good life, and he was living in a dirt lot with Marri.

He just wanted to drink his life away and not have to deal with the pain anymore. He wanted a way out of this situation. It hit him hard, and he didn't know what to do. He thought, *There has to be a better way to deal with this.*

When he got back to the dirt lot, he saw that Marri was reading the Bible, and then he said in his head, *That's it. I'm going to teach Marri the right way to deal with things. I'm going to teach her to be her best in any situation. I'm going to read the Bible to her so she could be a better person to others.*

CHAPTER 12

The next day was the first day of school, and John woke up early to make Marri a special breakfast for her special first day at a public school. He was very happy that she was so excited to meet new friends. After they had breakfast and prayed together, they walked to school together.

She asked him on the way to school, "What do you think about God?"

"I don't know who he is, but I want to learn more about him and what he did for the world. On Saturdays, there's a potluck at the church. I want to go eat and get some more information about the church."

"I want that too. I'm very excited to find out more about him."

John loved how his relationship with Marri had grown stronger and stronger every day. He could tell her just about anything. When they got to school, she saw how many people were there and got scared. She asked if he could walk her to her class and meet her teacher. He told her of course he would.

She held his arm really tight all the way through the hallways of the school. John felt so proud of himself of how his daughter needed him more than anything else.

He looked down. "I will always be there for you, no matter what."

They made it to her class, and Marri saw that her dad wasn't the only parent there. It made her feel better. They walked around her classroom, and he saw her eyes light up with excitement. The room had a bunch of drawings, and her classroom was lit up with colors and pictures of animals from zoos and other places around the world. John realized that this was where she should have been all along. She didn't need to be away from other kids. She needed to be with kids her own age and in her own grade. He wanted her to grow up and have friends she could trust and one day have her own kids and her own life. He just wanted her to be happy, and he never let her do what she wanted. It was always the way he wanted her to live her life.

That was about to come to a stop. It wasn't about him now, the money and all his so-called friends. He had the only person who meant the most to him, his daughter, and he will have to show her how to live a normal life.

He kissed her on the head. "Have a wonderful day. I will be here to pick you up right after school."

John needed to find a job, so he left the school and felt like nothing could stand in his way. For the first time in his life, he thanked God for the way he was feeling. He didn't know how to pray, but he understood that praying to God and giving him thanks would help him and Marri down the road.

He walked a few blocks from the school to see what was around so he could find work. John just needed a job where he could make just a little money to save so he could get a place for them. He walked past a small, local breakfast place that had a dishwasher posting on the window.

He walked in and asked to talk to a manager about the position. It was busy in there, and the manager was slammed in the kitchen cooking.

He told John, "I'm going to give you an interview while I'm working in the kitchen, but you have to be fast about it."

"I'm ready when you are."

He asked John about his background and inquired if he had any experience in the kitchen or restaurants before. John told him no. He did not want to lie to this guy about who he was, so he decided to tell him the truth. He told him his full name and said who he was. He also told him that he and his daughter were homeless, living down the street in a dirt lot. He said how broke he was and how he barely had food and water for him and his daughter.

While telling his story, John was in tears. "I have nothing. I don't care how much the job pays. I just need the money for my family."

The guy was honestly touched about John. He also knew who he was. "I could only pay in cash. It isn't a lot of money, and I only posted the job because I need a dishwasher for the end of my busy season, which is only about a month left."

"I will work my heart out for you, and I won't let you down."

"You have the job. It starts tomorrow at five in the morning."

"I will be there. Is it possible for me to leave to get my daughter ready for school and then come back to finish my job?"

"That's fine, but you won't get paid for the time you are gone. And you will have a lot of work to do when you get back." The man understood what he was going through. "You are a good man for staying strong. And if you need anything, I will do what I could to help you out."

John broke down in tears. "Could I pray for you?"

The man said he could. John began to pray for the man, thanking God for the man helping when he needed it the most.

The man told John, "Nobody has ever done that for me." And he began to cry as well.

John said, "Praying has been helping me get through the rough times that I have been going through."

The man had to get back to work, so he told John to be there at five in the morning the next day for his first shift.

"I will be here before five." And John left to go back to his place to finish fixing it up.

He wanted to surprise Marri and tell her that he got a job. So he started fixing up the place. He wanted to build a roof so they wouldn't get wet when it started to storm. He walked around the lot, looking for bigger branches and palm tree branches for the roof. While he was finding branches, he happened to see something shining in the dirt under some branches.

He started to dig and realized it was a gun that still had bullets in it. He knew it must have been used in a shooting because he wasn't in the best of neighborhoods. He kept it, and he was going to put it in a place where nobody could find it. It could come in handy if someone tried to rob him, or he could use it as protection for his family.

It was almost time to go pick Marri up from school so he finished up cleaning and fixing up the place. He walked to get her from school. John was feeling very happy about how the day went, and he started thinking of what he could buy his daughter with the money he would be getting from his job.

He got to the school. He waited outside the class to see how her first day at school was. The bell rang, and Marri came out smiling and laughing. She was slowly walking with a little girl whom she had met in class. It was good to see Marri having a great time in school and finding friends.

She ran up to her dad and gave him a huge hug. She told him that she had one of the best days in her life and how much she learned about planets, animals, and other things. She kept talking the whole way back to their place.

He was so happy that she got to experience school and being with kids her own age. When they got back to the dirt lot, he showed her what he had done with the place and told her that he got a job washing dishes in a restaurant.

She was so happy. "This was the best day I've ever had."

John told her, "There will be more to come."

CHAPTER 13

The next day, John got up feeling refreshed and positive about life and how things were becoming better for them both. He got up extra early so he could get ready for work and make sure Marri had everything she needed to get ready for school. He wrote her a letter, telling her to make sure she had something to eat and she was ready by the time he got back from working to take her to school. He wanted to be there early so he could impress his boss.

He got to work about fifteen minutes early, way before anyone else showed up. He started picking up the trash that was around the building. He noticed a lot of graffiti was on the side of the building. And when his boss showed up, he wanted to ask if he could do some painting for extra money or just additional hours.

His boss showed up and saw him picking up the trash around the building. "Good job. This neighborhood and all the gang activity is bringing down my business. I tried calling the police, but they couldn't do anything about it. So I didn't bother doing anything about it."

"Have you thought about moving your business to a better side of town because it looks like you get a lot of business in the mornings?"

"It does good business, but I can't stay open all day because it gets bad at night and I don't want people getting robbed outside my business because they won't come back."

John said, "At one time, I had so much money that I didn't know what to do with it. If only I knew then what I know now, I would be helping people, and I would have paid to help move your business to a better side of town because people come every morning to eat your food."

"I would love to move. You're a good-hearted man," the owner replied. "What happened to you was wrong, and I wish you could be in a better place than you are now."

"I know it will get better because I have been reading the Bible, and it tells me that things will get better for the ones who believe in God. I believe God will make things better for my daughter and me."

After the long talk he had with his boss, it was time to get to work.

His boss told him, "My last dishwasher couldn't keep up, and I had to get rid of him.

John said, "It won't be a problem. I know I can keep up and do a good job because my daughter needs this money to eat and get clothes for school."

"How are you bathing yourself?"

"I haven't showered in a few days. Neither has my daughter."

The man never had been in the situation that John was in. "You could use the bathroom here at work to wash up, and you could use the water hose at work if you need to. But the outside water isn't that good to drink from. On this side of town, everyone's drinking water isn't that good."

"Thank you for all the help you've been showing me. It's good to see other people helping those who really need it. Once I get back on my feet, I'm going to do more to help people who need the help and show people we can get help from others who care."

The man was impressed with who John was and was very thankful that he got to meet John as this person and not the person he once was.

John told him, "I'm upset about the things that have happened to me, but at the same time, I'm thankful that they happened because I would have never been able to really see who I am as a good father and person to other people. This is God's way of showing me who I really am."

John helped his boss open the restaurant because people were already standing outside, waiting to come in and eat. He went back into the kitchen and saw a bunch of dishes that were dirty, and he began to wash and clean dishes. Another job of his was to make sure, after a customer left, to clean the tables and wipe them down for other customers to sit down and eat.

He had a lot of duties as a dishwasher. It was a lot of work, but he was thankful to be working there and to have an opportunity to make a new friend and have someone to talk to, even if it were not going to be for long. His job only paid for four hours a day, and his boss told him that he would give him $100 a week, which was more than he was giving the other guy before him.

John was happy to get that, so he worked his butt off for that money. He never had a job that he had to do labor for his whole shift, so had to really work hard and learn new things to get the job done. He never stopped working the four hours he was there, and he kept asking his boss if there were anything else he could do to help out other people who worked there.

That man was stunned on how good of a worker John was, and the other people saw he was laboring hard. So they decided to work hard too. It was one of the man's best workdays of his business, and at the end of the workday, he gave John an extra $20 for his hard work.

Everyone there knew who John was, but they didn't care. They saw him as a hard worker and a good man. John made sure everything was cleaned and the floors were swept and mopped before he left. His boss had never seen his restaurant that clean before.

John had a few more hours before Marri got out of school, and he was so tired from work that he went back to the lot to take a nap. On his way back to his place, a group of young men who looked like gang members approached John. They harassed John because of a color he was wearing.

They asked John, "What gang are you from?"

John told them, "I'm not from any gang. I'm just on my way home from work."

They surrounded him. "Empty your pockets."

"I don't have anything."

"You're lying."

One man grabbed him from behind and started going through his pockets. They found the $20 that his boss gave him and threw him on the floor. "Thanks for the twenty dollars. Go back to wherever you came from and not come back in our hood."

John never had to deal with this kind of stuff before. He was so mad that he worked so hard for that money, and just like that, it was gone. Even though he had a job, he would have to stand on the corner to ask for money again.

As he walked back to his place, he thought, *If I had that gun on me, those guys wouldn't have taken my money.* He got back to his place and grabbed the gun. He said he was going to keep it on him at all times, but if he got caught with it, he might have to go to jail for a long time if the gun were used in a shooting.

So after long thinking and being mad, he decided to leave it behind and put it back where he got it from, his safe place. He left his place and walked to get Marri from school, making sure those guys wouldn't see him on his way to get her. John didn't want to run into those guys again, so he went a different way to get her from school.

When he got there, she came out of her class smiling. Her teacher was with her and told John that they needed to talk. John thought he was in in trouble and worried that Marri might have said something about what had happened to them.

He was surprised to find out that her teacher wanted to tell him about how great Marri was and how she got so excited to learn and wanted to learn more and more each day. He told her that she had a great, open mind and she asked questions every day about everything. She had never seen a kid so excited to learn in all her teaching in that school.

That made John's day so much better that she was learning everything she could. On their way back, they stopped by an ice cream place, and John had just enough money to buy her an ice cream cone for her hard work at school. She asked about his day, and he told her that things went well. He didn't want to tell her about being robbed for his money, so he didn't.

He told her that he wanted to read her some more stories from the Bible before she went to bed. She was so excited to learn more about God. She had a project to do for homework, a show-and-tell project. She wanted to take the Bible to school and tell the other kids about what they were reading about.

He told her, "That's a great idea. Kids need to learn more about God if they don't know about him."

When it was time to go back to their place, John told Marri that he wanted to go to bed early because he was so tired and wanted to get a full night's rest so he could do it all over again. On the way back, she couldn't stop talking about school and how exciting it was. John told her, if she wanted to, when she got older, she could go to college like he did and learn more. When he was in college, he learned about business and how to run a business. He never got to enjoy it and have fun.

"Just have fun in life and do what you believe that God wants you to do."

When they got back, John sat down with her, pulled out the Bible, and began to read and read to her, filling her mind and teaching her what he thought he was reading meant.

CHAPTER 14

After a great night's sleep, John woke up early again and went to work. This time, his boss was there with some paint buckets.

"Could you help start with some painting?"

"No problem. I was going to say something to you the other day about cleaning up this building."

His boss told him, "Your talk with me yesterday really opened my eyes on how I thought of people in this neighborhood. Not all people are bad. You pretty much changed my life, and now I can see the good in people and not the bad."

John hugged him. "Not all people are bad. Everyone has a story, but if they don't tell it, nobody would know who they really are."

As they started painting, other people passing by saw them painting and started to help. His boss was shocked that the community was coming together to help out.

One guy said, "It was about time you painted this."

And they all laughed. It was time to open up the restaurant, and John helped clean up the painting and told the owner that he would help him open up the store. The man had so much fun painting and talking to people that he forgot what time it was. The people were waiting to eat. So both John and the owner rushed to get the store open, and people saw that they were painting and told them to take their time.

John made such a difference in his boss' life in two day, more so than anyone else had. His boss told him, because of him, he was a better person and got to know his customers on a personal level and do more in his community. John felt good about himself because he was changing another person's life as he was transforming his own life as well.

After finishing his shift, John needed to make more money. He knew he had a few more hours until he had to pick up Marri. So he went back to his place, got his sign, walked to the corner, and stood out there for a while until he got enough money to feed Marri. He wasn't going to get paid for another week so he knew he needed something now.

After standing outside for over an hour, he only got a few bucks, barely enough to get some kind of food, but it was something she could eat, but not him. He decided to come back after he got Marri from school. Maybe he would have better luck. He folded up his sign and tucked it under his shirt so nobody would see it when he went to get her from school.

Once again when he got there, she was so excited to tell him about her whole day at school. John wanted to hear everything she had to say because she was so happy and he wanted her to stay that way in their time of sadness. He told her that he would have to work some extra hours, but he was really going to stand on the corner and ask for money. He didn't want her to know he was begging people for money. She told him it was okay because she had some things to color in a book her teacher gave her for being good at school.

They got back to their place, and John made sure she was taken care of before he left. He walked back out to the corner, took out his sign, and just waited for someone to give him some money. He stood out there for about another hour. It was getting really hot, and he needed some water to drink. He didn't have any water at his house either so he knew he would have to buy some soon. He didn't want to drink the neighborhood water because he couldn't afford to get sick from it.

A convenience store was right across the street, and he saw a few guys standing in front of the store begging for money. He figured that might be a good place to ask for help. He went over there to see if someone could help him out.

He went inside the store and asked the clerk, "Can I get a cup so I could get some water?"

She replied, "Cups are only for customers and not begging people."

So he went outside to ask for help. He asked and asked, and nobody would help him. Time was running out, and he knew he needed to get some water and food soon, or they wouldn't have anything at all. The store was across the street from where he was staying so he could keep an eye on Marri while he was there.

While he was standing out there, a truck pulled up with a bunch of guys. When they got out, he noticed it was the same guys who robbed him. They left the truck running and stood outside the truck, smoking and talking about going to rob and shoot someone. They looked at John but didn't recognize him at first, so they continued on with their conversation about how they were going to rob someone and possibly kill him for drugs and money.

John couldn't help but look at one of the men, who looked like he didn't want to go with them and kept telling them that he had a bad feeling about what they were going to go do. His crew kept telling him to stop being scared, saying it was his time to show them if he were down with them. If not, he would be on his own on the streets.

John went up to the man and said, "I'm homeless. Could you help me out so I could get some water and food for my daughter?"

The man looked right at him and told John, "Yeah, I can help you. I know exactly what you need." He went in the store.

John waited at the side of the store because he didn't want the other gang members to recognize him and try to rob him again.

Then the man came out of the store with a bag full of forty-ounce beers and gave one to John. "See, I told you I knew exactly what you needed."

John knew the beer would only make his situation worse, so he went back up to the man and tapped him on the shoulder.

The man turned around and yelled, "What you want, man? I just gave you a beer. Now leave me alone, or I will beat you up."

John asked, "Could I talk to you alone?"

"Fine!" The man walked a few steps so none of the other guys could hear him.

John told him, "As much as I would love to drink away my pain and suffering with a cold beer, I have a little girl I'm taking care of. She has nobody else, and I'm all she has. All I need is some water so she won't be thirsty." He pointed across the street where he was staying, and when he did so, Marri was standing out there, looking for him.

John started to cry. "If you could help me out, I would highly appreciate it."

The guy looked at John. "I'm sorry for judging you, and now I do know exactly what you need. I will be right back." And when the man returned, he had two jugs of water and four bags of food.

"Thank you. You have no idea how much I needed someone's help. Could I pray with you?"

The man said yes, but he didn't want his friends to see him. "Make it quick."

John bowed his head. "Thank you, God, for sending this man to help me in my desperate time of need. Please, God, protect this man on his path of life. Please protect him so nothing happens to him on the streets or when he goes out with his friends to do what they are going to do."

Then John took all the things the man gave him and went back to his place. The man stood there for a while, and then all his friends got in the truck and told him to get in or they were going to leave him.

The man looked at them. "I'm not going. I don't want to be a part of what you are going to do."

One guy asked him, "Are you sure you want to do this to us?"

He replied, "Yes, I don't want to join your gang anymore."

Another guy pointed a gun at him as they were pulling out and said, "You better watch your back because next time we won't be so nice of letting you go so easy."

Right there, the man thanked God, took off his colors, and went home.

CHAPTER 15

John went back to his place with all the food and water to show his daughter what the man gave them. She was happy because it had been a while since they had some good food to eat and have drinking water. John would have to make sure he put his food and water in a safe place to make sure nobody coming by would steal it from him. He had learned a lot of stuff since he had been on the streets. He had also taught Marri a lot about having to survive in the real world, but the most important thing he could teach her was how to care and love for other people.

John and Marri had lots of talks about life. He felt like he had to teach her how rough life could be because she could grow up to be someone who didn't care for others or cared who she hurt to get what she wanted. They had a great day, and John wanted to teach her more about the Bible before they went to bed. He had read to her every day and night, and the more he read, the more she wanted to learn.

The next day, John got up early like he usually did to make sure Marri had everything she needed before he went to work. He also looked at her drawings and things she did at school before he left. He just wished that one day things would get better for them and they would have a big house to go to. He still continued to write in the journal about everything that went on every day. He liked writing down everything because it reminded him that, no matter what happened to him on the streets, he still had his daughter to make sure he didn't do anything stupid.

He got to work early and started fixing up some things around his boss' building to help out like he usually did. His boss told him that he was the best employee he ever had and wished there were more people like him on the planet. John was truly blessed to have had an opportunity to work for his boss and be able to have changed his life and other lives around him.

After his four hours of work, John still had a few more days until he got his first paycheck so he had to go back to the corner to ask for money. He stood out there for a few hours, like he usually did. Then he decided to go back to his place before Marri got out of school. While he was walking back, he noticed a police car following him back to his place.

Right when he turned down the street to head home, the cop turned on his light. "Stop right there."

John did what he said.

The cop told him, "Keep your hands up." He got out of his car and asked John, "Put your hands on the hood of my car so I could check you for drugs or anything that was illegal."

John did what he wanted. The cop asked for some identification, and John gave it to him. He asked John to stay there while he ran his name. Then the cop came back and was being really disrespectful to John. The cop knew who he was and what he did to his ex-wife.

"Wife beater! You might have gotten away with it because you had money, but I'm not going to let you get away with it here." The cop took out his club and began to beat John.

John called out to the cop, "Please stop! I didn't do any of the things I was accused of."

The cop didn't believe him and just kept beating John. He hit John in his face, legs, and ribs really bad. The cop beat him so bad that John passed out from the pain. When he woke up, the cop was gone, and he was late to get Marri from school. John could barely get up on his feet, and he thought his ribs were broken. He had to wash all the blood off his face before getting to Marri's school, so he went to his place and used some of the water to wipe off the blood.

Then he tried to run to her school to get her. He ran as fast as his body would let him. He was coughing up blood and couldn't breathe well. He knew something was really wrong with him, but he couldn't afford to go to the hospital. Nor did he want to lose any time off work because he needed all the money he could get. When he got to her school, the teacher was there, waiting with Marri.

She asked, "Why are you so late?"

"I had an accident at work and fell. My coworkers wanted to make sure that everything was okay with me." John was trying so hard not to pass out from the pain or show her that he really needed to go to the hospital.

She gave John her personal number. "If something like this ever happens again, you are to call me. I wouldn't have any problem watching Marri for a while until you get there."

"Thanks for your help. I appreciate you for understanding."

Then they left and walked home.

Marri knew that something was wrong with him. "Are you okay?"

"I fell at work, and everything is okay."

But it really wasn't. He was in so much pain, and he really needed to have an x-ray of his ribs because he thought they might be broken. He really could not believe that this happened to him and wondered why people would do such bad things to other people without knowing the truth. He had been through hell because of what everyone thought he did but didn't do it.

He didn't want to feel depressed, but he was in a lot of pain and felt like he was back to where he was before. John was in so much pain that he could not do anything he once did before with Marri, but he wanted to still pray with her and teach her that there would be problems and they would run into bumps in the road. But he wanted her to learn not to give up.

He had one of the roughest nights he ever had. He was coughing up blood and didn't have anything to take for his pain. He started being really negative and in such a bad mood that he didn't even want to hear about Marri's day. He just wanted the pain to go away and wished none of this had even happened to him.

He went to bed in a bad mood. He didn't even tell Marri good night. He just lay in the corner and tried to lay on the side that didn't hurt and get some sleep. Marri knew her father was in pain, but she didn't know how she could help him.

So she just went over, gave him a kiss on his head, and told him, "Things will get better because God loves us and he will make things better for us."

The next day, he got up later than he used to get up. He didn't want to get up and get ready for work because he was in so much pain, but he knew he had to get up and try to do his best. He got to work almost an hour late, and his boss was concerned and saw that his face was swollen and he was in a lot of pain.

He asked John what happened, and John told him the truth.

His boss was pissed and told John, "You should file a complaint against the police officer."

"It wouldn't matter because I don't know who he is or what his name is, just kind of what he looks like. It happened so fast that I could not do anything to protect myself."

His boss told John to take a few days off and said he would pay him for the two days off, but he was to come back healthy. His boss then gave him his paycheck for the week and told him to get some pain medication or something to help with the pain.

John thanked him for everything he had done for him. Then he left for a drugstore to get something that would help with the pain and swelling of his face. He got the medication he needed and went back to his place. He was in so much pain, and he needed it to stop. He took more than he was supposed to take, not enough to kill him but enough to take the pain away.

He had about three hours to go until he picked up Marri from school, so he laid down and passed out. He woke up just in time to get Marri from school. He actually felt a little bit better, but he was dehydrated from all the pills he took. So he drank most of the water, but since he got paid, he could get more on his way back from the school.

CHAPTER 16

On his way to get Marri from school, John could feel like he was getting some of his energy back, but still he was really weak. He knew he still needed to go to the hospital. He was still coughing up blood, but not as much as he did before. He knew he was getting better, but it would take a few more days for him to be way better and in an improved mood.

When he got to the school, her teacher could tell that he was better than before.

"Are you okay?"

"I'm going to take some time off work to recover."

"I can still help if you need it."

"Thanks, but I'm okay." He didn't want her to know about where they were staying or anything they were going through.

When they started walking back, John asked Marri, "Has your teacher been asking questions about what is going on?"

"Yes. She has been asking about how things are at home, and she said if you just fell at work or did something else happen, but i didn't tell her anything

"Good job. Please do not say anything. That could get me in trouble because they would try to come and take you away from me."

She didn't want to be away from her dad, so she promised she would not tell her teacher anything. John told her that he wanted to walk a different way home from now on so they could see more of the neighborhood, but he actually wanted to stay off the main streets just in case that cop decided to beat him again. He just didn't want Marri to see it if did happen again. It would take them an extra half hour to get home, but it was worth it to John so nothing could happen to him while he was with her.

He was thinking that he needed a backup plan if something did happen to him so she could be safe. She would have to go to CPS, and someone else would have to take care of her until she was old enough to take care of herself. He hated thinking like that because it hurt his heart to think that way, but it was better to be safe than sorry.

They got back to their place, and John couldn't help but think of how her life would be if he weren't around. *Maybe it would be better if I weren't around and she was with CPS.* He just wanted to make sure that she would be taken care of if he couldn't do his best to protect her and take care of her.

That night, he wrote a letter explaining that, if someone would find his daughter around, it was because he did something to himself that he would no longer be living. She would have to go to CPS so someone could take care of her.

After he wrote the letter, he explained to her that, if something happened to him, like he didn't wake up from a nap or if he were so sick that he couldn't move, she would have to go across the street and hand this letter to someone. He would call someone to come help him.

She understood what he was asking and told her, "Dad, I would do everything you asked me to do because I don't want anything to happen to you."

John felt sad because he didn't want to do anything to himself, but he knew she was better off in a house where she could have food and water every day, something he couldn't give her. He read her the Bible and told her to go to bed because he wanted to get a good night's rest.

He tossed and turned all night, just thinking of killing himself for Marri to have a better life. It was one of the toughest decisions he would have to make, but he made up his mind. He was going to kill himself the next day.

When he woke up, he had his mind set on it, but he was still thinking of when was a good time to do it. He didn't have to go to work so he had all day to think about what he was going to do. He was sad and angry at the same time because he did all he could do, and still things were bad, but then things were good. He knew things could be better in time.

He got her up and ready for school. "Do you have that letter I wrote last night?"

"Yes. I put it in a special place that only I know where it is and nobody else."

John walked her to school, just wanting her to know that he loved her very much and he would always be around whenever she needed him. He was thinking in his mind that she would be sad if something happened to him, but then she would be happy later in life when she had everything she needed.

They got to school, and John took an extra long time walking her to class. He just wanted to be with her as long as he could until it was time to kill himself. He watched her walk into class. Then he turned around and starting crying. Deep down, he didn't want to do this to himself, but he know it would be best.

As he was leaving her school, he walked and walked and walked. He stopped at a park and watched other people with their kids having fun, but he knew these people had a home and a family to go back to. So that made him sad. The only thing he wanted in life was for Marri to be happy and have everything she deserved in life. He did everything he could do. He tried his best to be the best he could be for her.

He sat at the park mostly all day, thinking about how he failed in life and knowing that killing himself was the only way out. He gave up and couldn't take it anymore. He was going to do it, and nobody could stop him.

It was time for him to walk back and get Marri from school. He cried the whole way there. He just kept telling himself that this was the only way and she was way better off without him. He got to her school, and she came out running to him, telling him about her day at school. She was so happy to be there and to be with her dad.

John just smiled and told her, "I'm happy you're happy. I know you will be much happier when you get older."

They walked home together, and he just listened to her, not really saying much because he knew what he had to do, but he didn't want to say anything or give her a hint about what he was about to do.

When they got home, John made the best dinner they ever had and told her about the letter again. He reminded her about it again and told her to make sure she brought it to the right people if anything were to happen to him.

"I will find responsible people who I will think can help."

He smiled. "I love you so much. I know you will be in good hands."

He read her the Bible for about an hour, and she listened to each word he said. Then she fell asleep. John tucked her in her blanket and kissed her on the head. Then he left to go get the gun that was in his safe place. He decided to shoot himself in the head, but he didn't want her to find his body. He was going to do it outside their place.

He got his gun and found a place where he could shoot himself. She couldn't find him right away but would find him on her way to school. He got on his knees and started to pray. He asked God to forgive him for what he was about to do, but asked him to watch over his daughter and keep her safe and to make sure she would be safe for the rest of her life.

He started to cry and then put the gun to his head. Then he closed his eyes and began to pray some more. Just as he was about to pull the trigger and end it all, he opened his eyes and saw Marri was standing in front of him in tears. He must have been loud looking for his gun and woke her up and she went looking for him.

She was asking him, "Why would you want to hurt yourself? I thought we were going to live together forever and we were going to get a house together and have a better life. You told me that you would never leave me ever."

He put down the gun and held her close. "I'm sorry. I wasn't thinking straight. I wanted to hurt myself so you would go live with someone and live a better life."

She held him tight. "The only life I want is with you."

Then they both walked back to their place. He threw away the gun, and they went to bed.

CHAPTER 17

The next day, John felt terrible for what he was going to do to himself. He felt like it was selfish of him to think that way, but he did promise that he wouldn't leave her, and he needed to keep the promise to Marri. He got up and made her a nice breakfast to thank her for saving his life, and he wanted to talk to her about how they were going to get through this together and have a big house and lots of stuff like he told her before.

She was just happy to have him, and she gave him a huge hug. "I know we could have all that stuff if we just stayed together."

It was the weekend, and she didn't have school. So they decided to go to the park and have a father-daughter lunch. So he packed up some food, and they walked to the nearby park.

She asked, "When we get there, could you swing me on the swing?"

"Of course I would."

She was so happy that they were going to spend the whole day together and have fun. This was what he really needed. He just needed to spend some good quality time with Marri and not have to worry about anything or anyone but her. They had a great time walking around the park, just talking about when they got money, like where they were going to eat or get whatever they wanted.

Marri told John, "All I want right now is to be with you and to take a nice, long shower."

John said, "Yes, now that would be great to take a shower and have some clean clothes to wear."

He thought to himself, *It's crazy how the small things in life mean the biggest to those who don't have them.*

He told her, "As soon as I get enough money, I would make sure we could get a hotel so we could wash our clothes and take a shower."

The more they talked about having things, the more he knew that he had to do something more to get more money so he could get a place for them. He had to find another job, but he couldn't work two jobs because he wouldn't have anyone to watch Marri. He would just have to figure it out as they went along, but he wouldn't give up again on her. So the best thing he could do was take it one day at a time and be the best father to her that he could. He thought to himself that how could he be so stupid, everything he could ever want in his life was right in front of him. All he ever needed was his daughter and she was the key to his happiness.

After their walk, talk, and playtime at the park, they walked back to their place. On the way, John was having so much fun talking and playing with Marri that he didn't notice that he was walking on the main street where that cop saw him and followed him back to his place and beat him up.

So they just continued on walking, having no fear of nothing but just talking away and having a great time together. They came to their block and started to walk down their street when he noticed at the corner of his eye there was a cop parked in his car across the street from where they had to go.

John grabbed Marri's hand and told her to hurry up and get home so he could make them a good dinner. As they started to get closer to their place, the cop saw it was John and began to follow him. John thought to himself, *If I had my gun, I would have to defend myself in front of my daughter.* And he knew, if he did that, the cop would probably shoot him or just beat him up in front of her. He didn't know what would happen if it came down to that so he was just hoping the cop would keep on going and leave them alone.

They got about a hundred feet from their place when the cop turned on his lights and told him to stop. John was thinking all kinds of things he wanted to do to this cop, but he also thought of what would happen to Marri if he just didn't do what the cop told him to do.

The cop got out of his car. "Turn around and look at me."

So John turned around and looked at him. It was the same cop that beat him up. He got closer to John, and John grabbed Marri and put her behind him because he didn't want her to see him beat up in front of her.

The cop saw marri and also saw behind him and saw that he was heading to the dirt lot and thought to himself, *Maybe that's where he is staying with his kid.* The cop reached behind him, where his club was, and when John saw that, he balled his fists at his side to let the cop know he was ready to protect his daughter.

The cop reached back and pulled out his wallet. "I'm sorry for what I did. I shouldn't have done that to you. I know it isn't like me to do things like that to people, but I just reacted to how everyone else saw you. I did what I thought was right at the time, but I know it was wrong. I want to give you some money so you and your daughter could get a hotel room and some new clothes or something." He pulled out $200. "Please take it as a gift for you and your daughter."

"Thank you. I want you to know I was set up. Never did I put my hands on a woman. She took everything from me and left me alone on the streets with my daughter." He continued, "Could I pray for you so God will keep you safe out on the streets because he kept to his word and protected the people he said he would?"

The cop told John, "Thank you for praying for me. That's what I need, forgiveness from God." They shook hands.

John hugged him. "I forgive you."

Then the cop got back in his car and left.

John looked down at Marri. "We got our wish. We are going to get a room, take a shower, and get clean clothes. But I want to go to the church for the potluck I heard about first. Then we will go to the hotel."

So they went back to their place, put on their best clothes, and walked to the potluck that was at the church that was down the street. When they got there, there was a lot of music being played and people singing. John and Marri were excited and had never seen such happiness and love. People were dancing and singing, and they had a lot of food there.

Marri had such a huge smile on her face. It was like she couldn't control herself from being so happy. He loved the fact that she loved God so much and wanted to learn more. Some very happy people welcomed them, and they were thankful to see new faces.

John introduced himself and Marri, and he couldn't stop talking to people there. He felt like he was at home and they didn't care who he was. They were just happy to have him there, and that was all that mattered to him. They had the best meal they had in a long time. Marri couldn't help herself, but she ate so much that she said she would be full for a few days.

The pastor of the church came up to them. "Welcome. Have you ever been to a church before?"

John told him, "No, we haven't, but we will be coming to this church from now on. We are homeless, but I have been reading the Bible to my daughter at night, and she loves it."

The pastor asked, "May I pray for you?"

John said, "Of course you could."

The pastor prayed for them, asking that God would protect John and Marri and make sure they got everything they asked for. It was like at the right time in their life that it would happen.

John told him, "We believe in God, and since we've started believing, God has been working in our lives and showing us that there was a brighter light in our dark times."

"Please come back tomorrow. I can show you just how good God is and how he could change anyone's life if he would just get saved and believe in his heart that God is real and lives in each and every one of us."

John said he would for sure be back tomorrow. "Thank you for treating my daughter and me like a human being and not like bums off the streets."

After they talked to the pastor, he hugged them and told them to be ready for what God was about to do for them in their lives. Then they left with full stomachs and full minds of what was to come and how God was going to work in them.

A hotel was not too far from their place, so they went back and gathered enough clothes to wash for a week. Then they went to the hotel. They walked down the street a few more blocks and came to the first hotel they could find. It was still in the bad neighborhood, but it was the best hotel they had been to in a long time.

John got a room for a few nights, which was half the money he got from the cop. For the first day, they went swimming and washed their clothes. They had a really good time that day, and when the day was over, before they went to bed, John still had enough time to read the Bible to Marri and tell her that he thanked God every day that he had her in his life.

CHAPTER 18

They got back to their place feeling better than they ever had before. John was thinking about how thankful he was to have Marri and God in his life. He was so full of love and energy, and he knew that this was just the beginning and there would be more happy times and memories to come.

John still wasn't 100 percent better from when the cop beat him up, but he was ready to go back to work to make money and people happy. He felt so much love from the people he worked with and talked to every day. He just felt like a whole different person all around. His life was changed in every way. He was no longer a money-hungry person who thought of himself. He could actually say he had a few friends who didn't care about how much money or how powerful he was. The people who knew the true John knew him as a kind, caring, and loving person who loved God and people around him.

Even though he didn't have all the things he once had, he still had his daughter and some friends to be there for him. And that meant a lot to John. He looked back at his childhood and couldn't remember his dad telling him that he loved him or even good job. He promised himself right there that he would never be like his dad or treat his daughter like his father did him. They were going to have a happy life filled with great times and adventures. His daughter was his life, and he just wanted her to grow up and live her own life and do what God had put him here to do.

John told Marri that he wanted to take her to a place where they could sit down and eat somewhere nice. He was so excited, but she asked him, "Are you sure you have enough money?"

"Don't worry. I have enough money for us to eat well."

So they got ready, and they starting walking down the street and found a little Chinese restaurant that had a lot of colors and played music. She thought it was pretty and cool and wanted to go eat there.

He said, "Okay, let's go. I've had Chinese food before and like it."

She had never had it before so it would be her first time. They went inside and sat down, and someone came up and took their order. He suggested she would have the beef and fried rice, and he would have the chicken and fried rice. They would have a few sodas. Both were excited because they hadn't had a dinner like this in a long time.

They sat and talked for a while until their food got there, and when it did, her eyes lit up because it was a huge plate of food, and his was about the same size as hers. They were jumping for joy because of their plates of food.

John stopped his daughter before he ate and told her he wanted to pray before they ate, like the pastor did at the potluck. She said okay, so they prayed. They prayed that God would protect her and keep her safe. Then they prayed that God would make sure that he would give John the strength to continue to make money and take care of his daughter. Then they said "Amen" and began to eat.

John noticed at first that his chicken didn't taste right, and he asked the waiter to come over.

"Is there something wrong with the chicken you serve to people?"

"Nothing is wrong with the chicken. We use different spices in our restaurant, so maybe that's what it is."

John said, "Maybe you're right. It has been a while since I've had this kind of meal." So he continued to eat it all.

By the time both got done, they were so full that they could barely walk. From the potluck and the dinner, they were good for about three days. It took them a long time to get back home because they were so full, but John's stomach was starting to hurt, and he was just thinking to himself that it was just the food and the fact that he ate way too much. So he paid no attention to it.

By the time they got back home, his stomach was hurting bad.

He told Marri, "I ate too much and just want to sleep it off."

"I'm tired too and want to lay down."

Both tried to sleep it off, but John was feeling terrible. He knew something was wrong with that chicken, but he thought, *If I could get some rest and drink some water, I would feel better by the next day.*

He looked down at Marri, and she was already fast asleep. So he knew it wasn't her food that she ate, or she would be feeling the same way.

Throughout the night, he tossed and turned because his stomach hurt so bad. He started to throw up all the food he ate, and he had to use the bathroom at the same time he was throwing up. Now he knew for sure something was wrong.

He started to sweat, and he got the chills. He was getting sick from the food he ate, and it wasn't getting any better. He threw up for hours until there was nothing left to come out. He couldn't even hold down water. Every time he would drink it, it would just come right back up. He could not keep anything down.

The next day, John was so weak that he could barely get up, but he got up to make sure Marri got everything she needed for school and then went to work.

When he got there, his boss asked, "Are you okay?"

"I ate some Chinese food from the place up the street, and I think I got sick from it."

His boss saw how sick he was. "Take the rest of the day off, take your daughter to school, and get some rest."

"That's the best thing I can do because I didn't sleep much at all last night."

John left, but on his way home, he stopped at the drugstore and used the last bit of his money on some stomach medicine. He drank the whole bottle. He knew he was going to throw up a lot of it, but hopefully some would stay in his system. He was so sick that he was burning up, but he kept saying he was freezing cold.

He got back to his home and told Marri he needed to lay down for like an hour. Then he would walk her to school.

"Are you okay?"

"Yeah. I'm just not feeling good from the food we ate."

John was pale. He had no fluids in his body. He was badly dehydrated. He laid down to try to get some rest. Marri could see how hot he was because he was sweating through his clothes, but he kept telling her how cold he was and said he needed more blankets to keep himself warm. He was running a fever of about 105 degrees, and he was still getting hotter. She didn't know what to do.

A few minutes later, John started shaking badly. His eyes roamed back in his head, and he began to have a seizure. She tried her hardest to get him to stop shaking, and she was trying to hold him to keep him still, but he couldn't stop. His body was shutting down, and he was dying.

It was then that she remembered to go across the street and ask for help if anything would happen to him. So she ran as fast as she could to get help.

She ran through traffic, almost getting hit by cars to get some help. She ran right into the convenience store. "Help! Help!"

The clerk asked, "What's wrong?"

She yelled, "My dad is dying, and he needs help!"

The lady called the cops and asked, "Where is your dad?"

She pointed over to the dirt lot where they were staying.

"Okay, the ambulance is on its way. Let's go over there to see if he is okay."

They both ran back over to John, now not moving or breathing. Marri was crying for her dad. John just laid there, not responding to anyone or anything. About five minutes went by, and they could hear the ambulance coming. So the lady ran out to the street and waved them down.

She pointed and said, "He's over here."

When they got to him, they saw he wasn't breathing, so they started CPR on him to get him breathing again. The cops showed up and took Marri back to their police car because they told her that she shouldn't be watching them try to save her dad.

They put John on the gurney and took him in the ambulance to the nearest hospital. The cops were asking Marri a bunch of questions about what they were doing there. She told the cop everything, saying they were homeless and had been living there for a while. She said that her dad was taking care of them.

The cop called for some help to go through their stuff, get their things, and take them with everyone to the hospital. A female cop showed up and helped them get the stuff from the lot. They found clothes, the Bible, and John's journal where he wrote down everything that had ever happened to him—from having all the money and his company, losing it to his ex-wife, and enduring everything that happened to them up to this point.

On the way to the hospital, the cop couldn't put down John's journal. She cried a lot as she read it. She looked back at Marri and told her, "You know everything will be okay with your dad. You know he loves you very much and would do anything for you, so he's going to fight this and get better for you."

Marri stopped crying so much. "I know. My dad is a very strong person, and he wouldn't give up one me."

CHAPTER 19

When they got to the hospital, Marri asked to see where her dad was, and they told her that the doctors were still working on him and didn't have any answers to her questions at this time. But they would get back to her as soon as they heard from the doctors.

So they waited for hours to hear back from the doctors and still didn't hear anything yet. A strange woman sat down next to Marri and started asking her questions about her dad and how they ended up in the dirt lot. The two police officers called CPS on John become he was living on the streets and they wanted to take her away from him. She asked her about what happened to her house and why they had to live on the streets. She told them they had to leave because his dad didn't have any more money. He tried and tried to make money, but he could not get a job. Then she told him how he did get a job, how she was going to school, and how her dad was taking her to school after going to work and picking her up every day.

The woman was surprised that John was doing all that. She just assumed he wasn't doing anything for Marri at all. "You will have to stay at a home for a few days to make sure you will be able to go back with your dad if he makes it through his sickness."

Marri told her, "There's no way I'm leaving my dad behind, and they can't take me away from him."

The doctor came out and said, "John is going to make it. We just saved him in time. He has salmonella poisoning. He was about to die, but we caught it in time."

The doctor heard what she did and told Marri, "Thanks to you, your dad is going to live. Now that we know he is going to survive, we need to take you to the home."

"No! Where is my dad? I want to be with him."

She overheard someone say he was in room 215 in recovery, and she took off running down the hall. She ran down the hall, yelling, "Dad, where are you? I need you! Please, Dad, you sad nobody would take us from each other. Where are you?"

She ran down another hallway, yelling the same things, crying for her dad. John wasn't fully conscious, but he could hear her voice, and he started to talk back. But it wasn't loud at all because he was so weak from almost dying. Then he heard her again, yelling for him.

John opened his eyes and asked, "Marri, where are you? Daddy's right here."

Then she got quiet. She heard him but didn't know where he was.

Then he said it again, "Marri, where are you? I'm right here." He was down the next hall.

She ran as fast as she could, yelling, "Daddy, I'm coming to you."

He was yelling right back, "I'm in here."

She finally got to his room and saw him on the bed with all kind of tubes going through him. She looked at him. "I found you, Dad. I know you wouldn't leave me."

Then he started to cry, and she saw him tearing up.

"Is it windy in there?"

"No, baby. I'm crying because I'm happy to see you."

"I know you've been crying the whole time. I just didn't want you to know I knew."

John gave her the biggest hug he could give her, but he was so weak that he couldn't hold her tight. Then the doctor, the CPS lady, and the cops came in the room. The CPS lady told John who she was and said she had to take Marri for a few days until he got better. Then he would have to go in front of a judge to see if he were fit enough to take care of her.

John asked, "What do you mean? I've been taking care of her my whole life, and if it weren't for me getting sick, nobody would have known we were out there. We minded our own business and stayed away from most people, just trying to survive on the streets."

The woman cop who read his journal told him, "I understand everything that happened to you. I promise you that I will make sure that your daughter will go to the home until you get better for her. I will take extra care of her, even after I got off work. Just hang in there. I couldn't help but read your journal. I was so touched by the things you had to do for your family. It's amazing. The story you wrote needs to get out, and people need to hear it."

John said, "All I need you to do is take extra care of my daughter until I get better." Then he looked down at Marri and kissed her on the head. "I'm going to get 100 percent better. I will get out and come see you as soon as I leave here."

Then they took her away, and the doctors stayed to take care of John. They told him what had happened to him and what he needed to do to get better. They told him he would be in there about a week to fully recover to 100 percent.

John told them, "I will do what you want me to do, but I'm leaving to go see my daughter when I'm done."

The doctor said to just get some rest. They would be back tomorrow to check on him and take blood samples and other stuff to make sure everything got better and he got stronger. John told everyone to get out because he needed his rest and he didn't want to be bothered.

John was so tired and weak. He still needed his rest. The doctor gave him something to help him sleep, and John was knocked out. He slept for eleven straight hours. When he woke up, he was starting to feel better.

He called for his nurse. "Could you bring me some water?"

She brought him some water.

He asked, "Why is it so loud in the hallway?"

"Reporters and TV crews are trying to get in here to see you. They heard about your story on the news about you being homeless on the streets with your daughter. They want to know more about your story."

"I don't want to talk to anybody. I just want to see my daughter. Can you tell them to leave because I don't want to tell them anything?"

She went in the hallway and asked them to leave. Later that day, the woman cop came in the room and told John that she shared his story with a friend of hers. It became so popular in the last ten hours that people wanted to hear the full story about what he had been through.

"You are inspiration to me, and I just wish you would tell your whole story because people really need to hear how you survived out there and what was going through your mind."

"I will think about it."

She told him as she was walking out the door, "It would look better in court if you told your whole story. They would know about the true you."

John thought about that after she left. It was the people who judged him the first time. Now if the people wanted to hear his story, he told himself that he would have to think about it for a few days to make sure he could trust people again. He needed more rest, strength, and food. He was getting fed well while he was in there. He just wished Marri could be enjoying the same food he was.

The woman cop came back. "I've been checking up on Marri. She's doing well and eating a lot."

He laughed. "That's my girl."

"You're doing well and getting better. You will be getting out soon to see her. She misses you a lot and wished you would come see her sooner."

"I'm trying to get all my strength back, and I will have it soon. I thought about what you said. I think it's a good idea if people hear my story. By sharing my story on the streets to strangers, I am able to save some people's lives and change them completely. So if this is what God wants me to do, I will do it."

"I know someone who would come in here and record you, and you could tell her everything that happened. They could make it into a book and sell it."

John agreed for the woman to come in the next day, and he would tell her everything.

The next day, the woman cop came back with her friend that she told him about. She started to record him. John closed his eyes and began to tell her everything. This went on for hours. John opened up like he never did before, and when it was all done, John felt so good, like a huge boulder had been lifted off his shoulders.

He knew he did the right thing by telling his story. Then he looked back and said, "I guess everyone has a story that just needs to be told. Maybe this story could help out a lot of people who need help in the world."

CHAPTER 20

John was almost 100 percent better, and it was almost time for him to get out of the hospital and go to see Marri for the first time in a week. He was nervous to see what the judge and people would say on how he wasn't a good father by letting Marri go through what he had to endure. But all he wanted to do was be with his daughter, and that was it.

He had about two hours until it was time to go to court. A few people pitched in and bought him a nice suit so he would look nice in court. He cut his hair, shaved his beard, and took a shower. It had been a long time since he cut his hair and beard because he didn't care about what he looked like. He was just providing for his family.

When he got all done and put on his suit, he looked like a whole new person. He looked like what he did before he was homeless. People looked at him and were in shock because they had never seen him look like that before. After he was all ready to go, he went back in his room, got down on his knees, and began to pray.

A few people saw him praying and decided to go in the room with him. They put their hands on his back and began to pray for him. About ten minutes went by of praying with and for John.

Then he stood up, hugged everyone, and told them, "Thanks for all your prayers and support, but now it's time to get my daughter back."

As he was leaving his hospital room, he saw a bunch of reporters trying to get some pictures and information from him on what had been going on with him and where he have u been att for all this time after your divorce. The only thing John said was that he already shared his story with someone and it would be told when the time was right. He got in his cab and took off for the courthouse.

It was about thirty minutes away from the hospital, and he didn't want to be late. The cab driver got him there in time. He told the cab driver to drop him off by the side because he saw a bunch of reporters and didn't want to talk to them. So he went in the side entrance.

As he was going through the metal detectors, someone saw him and tried running to get a picture of him, but the cops at the door stopped them. They weren't allowed in the court building with all their equipment so they had to stay outside and report the news, which they did.

John had a public lawyer that they gave him. He had some bad experiences with lawyers so he told him that he wanted to talk for himself and explain his story to the judge. If he would not allow him to do that, he would find someone else to do his job. The lawyer told John that it was not a problem, and they went in the courtroom.

When they walked inside, John saw Marri, and she was in a pretty dress. He starting crying.

He looked over and told her, "You look very pretty."

"You look better."

Both laughed, and then the judge told them that they had to begin.

John looked behind him and saw the woman cop, his boss and coworkers, and even people from his church. He even saw the ex-gang member that he helped at the convenience store there as well. Just about everyone he helped on the streets were there. His friend Frank and his girlfriend were there as well. The only people who didn't show up were his parents, but he already knew they weren't going to appear.

He was overwhelmed that he had that many people there and he touched so many people's lives as he was going through the hell he endured. He felt so much love that he actually had people who cared and wanted to see him with his daughter.

The judge told them that they had to start, and they commenced. The CPS lady was trying to put Marri in foster care. She wanted to make the judge and jury believe it wasn't right for John to have her.

She would go first. "What John did was wrong and cruel. No child should be out on the streets in that environment and have to survive in those circumstances. She needs to be in a home where she will have the proper clothes, food, water, and love that she deserves." She went on and on for about another twenty minutes about how horrible John had been to his daughter. "Not only should he not be able to have her, he should go to jail for child abuse."

Then it was John's turn. He got up there, looked around, and said, "I just want to thank everyone who came out to support me, and if I were such a bad person, I wouldn't have all this support."

Everyone who was there for him got up and starting clapping.

The judge told them, "You must be quiet, or you will have to leave."

Then John went on to tell his story. "I once had everything I could ask for, and just that fast, it was taken away from me. I lost my wife to cancer. I never should have gotten remarried, but it happened. Being on the streets wasn't the hardest thing. I had time with my daughter, but I didn't want to be without her because that was all I had left in my life. My daughter saved me from fully breaking down and giving up. Because of her, I found God, and she wanted to learn more about God on her own. So I read the Bible to her every night. Because of the light that shined in her, it made me want to live and be a better father to my daughter. I owed everything to her, and without her in my life, I would be lost and probably no longer on this planet."

He asked the judge, "Please don't take away my light because, without my light, I wouldn't be able to see my way in life."

He had just about everyone in tears, even the judge.

The judge told him, "Please step down. Is there anyone else who would like to talk on behalf of John?"

First, his boss got up. "I owe John more than a thank you. I owe him a lifetime of thanks and love." He told them how John came into life a honest man and worked hard for him. He treated everyone with kindness and love. He was the best man he had ever met, and he believed that John was an angel sent from God because he had changed his life completely.

Then the gang member stood up and said he was about to go do something bad to some other people, and then John came into his life. Not only did he talk him out of going to do some really bad stuff to other people, he convinced him to buy a bunch of food and water for him.

Then everyone laughed, but he said, "When it all came down to the end, John saved my life and got me to quit the gang I was in."

Then the cop lady stood up. "I got to see where John and his daughter were living, and for being a homeless man, he sure was very organized and clean. He had all their clothes folded, and all his food was well put away. He had more stuff than some houses I've been in on that side of town. He might not have had a house with doors and running water, but he sure had a home. In my eyes, he's been keeping his daughter well taken care of. I've seen places way worse than his situation. I've never seen a case where not only was the kid healthy but she was going to school on top of being homeless." That was a first to her.

The judge was very impressed with all the support that John had from the community and friends. "I'll take a ten-minute break and be back with my decision."

After the ten-minute break, the judge had everyone stand up to tell them her decision. She looked at John. "In my ten years of being a judge, I have never had a case like this one before. I want to thank you, John, for showing me that there are people out there who would do anything for their families and would go to the end of the earth to see their children happy and not their own lives. You are an amazing father and a good friend to the people who loved you."

She finally said, "I give you full custody of your daughter, but you have to go through a few housing programs that will put you both in a government housing program where you can have a temporary place until you get fully on your feet."

After she said that, everyone cheered for John and tried to give him a hug, but he just wanted to hold his daughter first. She ran up to him and jumped in his arms like she never had seen him before. She was so happy to be with him, and he was exhilarated that he could be with her again.

John told everyone thanks for the support he got from them. "I am so thankful to have friends who really care about me." Then he told the judge, "Thank you for not taking my light way from me. I don't have any problems seeing now."

She smiled. "It was an honor to have met someone as special as you are. I wish you many more years of happiness to you and your family."

"Thank you. I will be doing my best to watch my daughter grow until she is the woman her mother would be proud of." Then he turned to his friends and celebrated with them.

On the way out of the courtroom, the cop lady came to him. "I want to let you know that my friend, the one who recorded your story, had talked to an editor. They want to make your story into a book. I will stay in contact with you and let you know more about what would happen."

He thanked everyone and told them, "God bless." Then he left down the hall with his daughter.

A year would go by, and his story was told nationwide. His book was a best-seller four months in a row, and there was talk about a movie that would tell his whole story.

One day, John was walking downtown on his way to a book signing at one of the best bookstores in town, and he stopped to look at a poster on the wall of him holding his book with the title "best-selling book" on it. He began to look back at everything and everyone who was in his life. He stood there for a few minutes and thanked God for everything he put him through.

Then he looked up to the sky and said, "I knew you would be there for me." He smiled and walked to his book signing.

John made a lot of money from his book and got everything he wanted again. He bought a big house just for him and Marri. He opened a homeless shelter and fed the homeless twice a week. He started a program that helped homeless people find jobs and the help they needed. He had the ex-gang member run it all. He bought a building on a great side of town, opened a restaurant for his old boss, and made him owner of it. For all the people who worked for him, he gave them all raises because it turned out to be one of the best breakfast places to eat in town. He gave the cop lady a percentage of his book earnings because she believed his story would be great.

He later found out that Michelle and Derek got a divorce. Derek took everything from her, leaving her with nothing. He sold the business and moved out of the country.

One day, John was at his new house, and he heard the doorbell going off. He walked and opened the door. It was Michelle, and she was crying.

"I've lost everything, and I'm having a hard time trying to find work and a place to go. I'm so sorry for what happened. If you could find it in your heart to forgive me, I will do anything you ask me to do."

"I forgave you a long time ago. I will help you."

He looked down and saw Marri right there, looking up at him with a horrible face.

He looked back at Michelle. "Wait right here. I will be back."

Then he walked in his room and grabbed his Bible. He went into the kitchen and got a jug of water and a loaf of bread. He went back to the door and gave it to her.

She asked, "What the hell is this? I asked for help."

John looked at her. "Do you see everything I have now?"

"Yes."

"I got all this from that Bible and a loaf of bread. I didn't even have the jug of water. I was just being nice and threw that in."

"Please help me." She put her foot in the door.

"Okay, I will let you in, but you have to step back and take off those shoes because they are dirty and I don't want that in my house."

She stepped back and took off her shoes. Then he slammed the door in her face. She started banging on the door, calling him all kinds of names.

Then he got on his speaker and said, "If you don't leave my property, I will let the dogs out of their cages."

Marri looked at him. "You're really going to let the dog out on her?"

He smiled. "I never put them in their cages, and I'm not sure how she got to the door without them getting her in the first place."

She grinned back at him and gave him a high five. Then she looked up at John and asked what do we do now, he replied the world is yours, you can do anything you want to do.

Printed in the United States
By Bookmasters